LOUD BLACK GIRLS

Also by Elizabeth Uviebinené and Yomi Adegoke

Slay In Your Lane

Slay In Your Lane: The Journal

LOUD BLACK GIRLS

20 Black Women Writers Ask: What's Next?

ELIZABETH UVIEBINENÉ
and
YOMI ADEGOKE

4th Estate • London

4th Estate
An imprint of HarperCollins*Publishers*
1 London Bridge Street
London SE1 9GF

www.4thEstate.co.uk

First published in Great Britain in 2020 by 4th Estate

1

A catalogue record for this book is available from the British Library

ISBN 978-0-00-834261-6 (hardback)
ISBN 978-0-00-834262-3 (trade paperback)

Printed and bound in CPI Group (UK) Ltd, Croydon

MIX
Paper from
responsible sources
FSC™ C007454

This book is produced from independently certified FSC paper
to ensure responsible forest management

Find out more about HarperCollins and the environment at
www.harpercollins.co.uk/green

Contents

Foreword

Black British women have always had a lot to say about everything, but until recently our voices rarely made the transition from our personal conversations into the public sphere. However, the days when our absence as writers from discussing the important issues of the day are, hopefully, coming to an end. Painfully, perhaps shamefully, it was a silence that seemed to go unnoticed by everyone but ourselves.

While there is a long heritage of black women publishing in Britain going back to Phyllis Wheatley in the eighteenth century and Mary Seacole in the nineteenth century, books have nonetheless been few and far between. This appears to be changing, and we are starting to be heard on an unprecedented scale through the recent publication of several bestselling and hugely acclaimed non-fiction books that have hit the headlines such as *Slay In Your Lane* by the editors of this anthology, *Brit(ish)* by Afua Hirsch, *Don't Touch My Hair* by Emma Dabiri, *I will not be erased* by *gal-dem*, *Sensuous Knowledge* by Minna Salami and *Why I'm No Longer Talking to White People about Race* by Reni Eddo Lodge. Black women are also being sought for our opinions as journalists and essayists in the media. The barriers that previously existed seem to be slowly dissolving, in no small part due to the power of our collective voices on social media where we've discovered both a global and local appetite for what we have to say. Today we are adding fresh perspectives and ideas to the intellectual conversations of our times – society, politics, culture – and always from the unique specificities of our experiences and intersecting identities. It's not that we've never had champions speaking at every level from and about our communities before, but rather that we haven't had enough of them. And because it's challenging to access records from the pre-Internet past, dispersed and under-archived as they are, even when the will is there, the legacy remains unknown. Thankfully, today's essayists, speakers, writers and opinion-formers are leaving substantial digital documentation, which means that this new history-in-the-making will not be so easily erased or hard to access for future generations. One hopes that so long as the Internet shall live, the archive of our lives and contributions will survive.

We black British women are minoritised in Britain in the twenty-first century on account of our skin colour and gender, primarily, but *Loud Black Girls* shows that we are fighting back through the power of essays that recontextualise the hegemonic structures of Britain simply by positioning black women at the centre of public discourse and therefore transforming the conversations. We have always valued ourselves, of course. We have always been at the centre of our own existence. We have always been as individualised as any other demographic, and the twenty writers in *Loud Black Girls* exemplify our endless possibilities as thinkers, creators, activists, challengers. The fact is that plurality, polyvocality, multiplicity – however we describe it – functions to counterbalance invisibility and reductionist stereotyping, and this anthology spills over with a thrilling range of voices. Among these pages you will find women writing about career paths, the ethics around influencers working with brands and issues around social media; there are questions around black women's roles and voices in theatre, and the semantics and implications of labelling as it pertains to people of colour. We also hear about cultural and generational differences, as well as discussions of representation, isolation, and perspectives around sexuality, gender, family, violence, self-discovery and the future.

I so enjoyed stepping inside the minds of these younger women who have so much to say, so much to express, so much to challenge. Yet we also have so much further to go, so much more to address and interrogate. Nobody can speak up for us, and each generation has to take on the challenge of speaking up for themselves. This is an exciting era; long may it continue. We are becoming known. We are being heard. Now is our time.

BERNARDINE EVARISTO
Writer, Booker Prize Winner 2019 and
Professor of Creative Writing, Brunel University
London

Introduction from Elizabeth

In 2018, Yomi and I threw a brunch in a private room at a London restaurant to celebrate the publication of our first book, *Slay In Your Lane*, bringing together a group of black women we had long admired. After the brunch ended a few of us moved to the main part of the restaurant to continue our conversations. Twenty minutes later we were 'kindly' informed that we were talking too loudly and asked to quieten down. When we looked around, we could see that the whole restaurant was filled with people talking very loudly, yet we seemed to be the only people being chastised. We looked at each other in disbelief, but we were not surprised; we immediately knew what was going on. We were the 'loud black girls'. Our presence had been felt and it wasn't welcomed; our voices were welcomed, but only when they were contained in a separate room and sadly our experience, while frustrating, wasn't isolated.

Being a loud black girl isn't about the volume of your voice; and using your voice doesn't always mean speaking the loudest or dominating the room. Most of the time it's simply existing as your authentic self in a world that is constantly trying to tell you to minimise who you are.

Meghan Markle, speaking on a Royal Foundation Forum panel in 2018, pointed out something that encapsulates exactly how I feel about having a voice. She said, 'What's interesting is, I hear a lot of people – when speaking about girls and women empowerment – you'll often hear people say, well, you're help-ing women finding their voices and I fundamentally disagree with that. Women don't need to find a voice, they have a voice, and they need to feel empowered to use it, and people need to be encouraged to listen.'

I couldn't agree more. It's like when we see a racist or sexist marketing campaign and as part of the backlash I've often heard people say, 'This is why they need to hire more black people or women, etc.' so these things don't happen. Yes, hiring is a factor but we have to also recognise that there are people who are cur-rently sitting in those rooms and don't feel empowered enough to use their voice.

The truth is that black women and girls are far too often pun-ished for using our voices. Every day we have to make choices between speaking up or walking away, and when we continuously choose silence we ultimately reach a point at which our core ends up screaming. How many times have you silenced yourself for fear of being labelled the loud black girl, or being 'too much'? How often have you found yourself over-analysing the space you're in to make sure it is a safe space to speak or be yourself?

To say we live in uncertain times would be an understatement, and as we enter a new decade, I'm even more conflicted about what real progress looks like for black British women. What does it mean to be a loud black girl? How do we take up a seat at the table and still speak in our authentic voices? What I do know for sure is that black women will always continue to find ways to use their voices to empower each other, their communities and be on the front lines of change.

Over the last few years I have found myself using my voice more than ever before, writing, speaking on panels, at events and in interviews. It used to make me anxious but now it's almost second nature, and ultimately it feels good. One of the reasons we wanted to create this book is to give a platform to the voices of black women in published work. The essays in this anthology are from twenty black British women who are using their voices to explore what it means to exist as a black woman in these turbulent political times.

I hope the pages that follow will be the spark you need to work out what you want to change about the world we currently live in, and how you will choose to use your voice. What ignites that fire is different for everyone: it may be activism in your local community, it could be journalism, it could be events, it could be dance . . .

Whatever you choose to do and to channel your voice into, always remember to exist loudly, loud black girl.

ELIZABETH

Introduction from Yomi

'Black women will always be too loud for a world that never intended on listening to them'
@WrittenByHanna

A few years ago, I stumbled across a blog post that changed my life. It was a short, now-decade-old piece by a New York-based blogger called Julian Abagond, on a phenomenon called 'The Three Bears Effect'.[1] The theory, created by another blogger called Aiyo, who blogged at the site *Black British Girl*,[2] suggested that many of the stereotypes aimed at black and Asian people were diametrically opposed, positing white people in the middle as 'just right' à la Goldilocks and the Three Bears. 'If blacks are cool, then Asians are nerdy,' Abagond explained. It went on – if black people are seen as less educated than white people, then Asian people are more. If black men have abnormally large manhoods then Asian men are stereotyped as theirs being particularly small and black people are deemed hypersexual compared to our regularly desexualised Asian counterparts.

One thought in particular stuck out to me, as it spoke about how these stereotypes affect women in particular: 'If black women are disagreeable, overbearing and loud, then Asian women are sweet, submissive and quiet.' I was in the formative stages of my awareness around race and racism, and the article blew my mind. It explained something I know well now, but at the time was a real revelation: minorities are only ever understood in relation to whiteness. Black people, black women in particular, are continually characterised as 'too' something, or 'not enough' something else, in a world where white men are the default. Everything else is considered a deviation or anomaly. As perfectly explained in another of Abagond's posts, 'If I draw a stick figure, most Americans will assume that it is a white man. Because to them that is the Default Human Being. For them to think it is a woman I have to add a dress or long hair; for Asian, I have to add slanted eyes ... The Other has to be marked. If there are no stereotyped markings of otherness, then white is assumed.'

One of the claims laid at black women's feet is that we're 'too loud'. In our first book, *Slay In Your Lane*, I write about how Elizabeth and I were referred to as the 'too loud, too black freshers' throughout university. But the question that we never had answered was: 'too loud and too black' for whom? Reading that blog a year or so later made things immediately clear: in a society built in many senses in opposition to who you are, how can you be anything other than 'too' something? Too much, too confident, too angry, too dark, too sexual, too loud, too bitter, too demanding. Black women are deemed 'too' something by virtue of existing, and even more so within spaces never created with us in mind. Silence and invisibility are considered the only remedies, and the next best thing is shrinking and assimilating as much as we can: talking more softly, wearing our hair straighter, anglicising 'difficult' names. But the game is rigged from the start. Despite attempts at being 'just right' we are still so often picked at, scrutinised and put to the side of the table.

Despite our alleged loudness, most black women are still not being heard in Britain today. So many of us have had our voices amplified and have 'slayed in our lanes', but the majority are still spoken over and defined externally. That is why with this book, we felt the need to reclaim that accusation of being 'loud' as a badge of honour. We are by no means loud enough – in the same way those before us ran so we could fly, we must shout so the generation after us can roar. Our first book was about the present and with this anthology we look to the future. In this, we raise our voices and shout over the stereotypes, misconceptions and continued attempts to author our own stories, so we can finally be heard on our own terms. #SlayItOutLoud

YOMI

References

1 Julian Abagond, 'The Three Bears Effect', Abagond [blog] (19/11/2010) <https://abagond.wordpress.com/2010/11/19/the-three-bears-effect/>
2 Aiyo, Black British Girl [blog] <http://blackbritishgirl.blogspot.com/>

ABIOLA ONI

Abiola is a Nigerian writer and winner of the inaugural *Guardian*/4th Estate BAME Short Story Award in 2016. We loved her short story '75' and we've been looking for an opportunity to work with her ever since we first read it. Here she writes warmly about her experience of being a black woman in Britain as a recent immigrant, part of 'the second great wave of black migration'. She eloquently reflects on her desire to prove herself, and her journey to self-awareness, spurred on by other black women who showed her that it is okay to be different.

Finding Myself In Britain

I was a fully-fledged adult when I moved to this country but I already knew the streets of London well.

From childhood until my mid twenties, I'd spent many summers in London: dancing at Notting Hill Carnival; walking up and down Oxford Street until my joints ached. I have particularly fond memories of wandering around the British Museum. There was always a free exhibition on Greek mythology in those days and I was utterly fascinated by tales of the Trojan horse, Medusa's head of snakes and Aphrodite's many lovers.

I was born in London but my family moved back to Nigeria shortly afterwards, and that was where I grew up. When I returned to England, it was for a postgraduate degree, and after a cold grey year in Manchester, with my degree clutched in my fingers, I moved down to the city of my birth in search of work.

At first, I wasn't called for many interviews, but it was shortly after the recession in 2008, I hadn't expected it to be easy. I dropped 'Lagos, Nigeria' off my CV, adopted a pseudo-British accent, and the interviews started pouring in.

I remember one of the recruiters I worked with saying I presented myself well. Why wouldn't I? I thought. She had read my CV – I had a bachelor's degree from the premier university in West Africa, a postgraduate degree from a top-tier university in England and two years of experience with a global consulting firm, albeit in the 'Nigerian office'. Of course I presented myself well.

You see, I was part of what David Olusoga has called the second wave of black migration in Britain. In his book titled *Black and British: A Forgotten History*, he describes a trend that started in the 80s – the migration of middle class, educated West Africans, immigrants mostly from Nigeria and Ghana. For my parents' generation, there was no defining moment, like Windrush in 1948. Perhaps this is why the narrative of black immigrants in the UK remained static? Perhaps the recruiter did not expect someone like me to have only recently migrated from Africa?

About six months after I started being called for interviews, I accepted a great job. I was one of the lucky ones. Most of my classmates who had moved down to London had to go back home. And so my real life in Britain began.

It wasn't too hard to settle in. My sister had moved to London years before, I had a few classmates from school scattered around the city. But for the first time in all my trips to London, I was exposed to more English people: to colleagues and new friends.

What struck me most was how little they knew about Nigeria, or even Africa in general. I knew so much about England, not just because I was born here but we'd been taught the history of Great Britain at school. And what we hadn't been taught at school, we'd learned through TV, through shows that I'd watched growing up, like *Carry On* and *Mind Your Language*. Naively, I'd thought people would know about us too.

There were the usual tired stereotypes – the email scammer jokes were rife – but there were other things that started to gnaw at me. When I told a colleague that my favourite cartoon show growing up had been *Dexter's Laboratory*, he seemed surprised that we'd owned a TV at all, let alone had cable television. Or the look on the face of a girl I met at a party when I said my father was an Imperial College alumnus. Or when a mixed race man I was on a date with told me I spoke so well.

I realised that to many, I was a unicorn.

Then there were the other black Brits, the second and third generation immigrants I met. They were wearier, less trusting of other races and British institutions. I understood where this was coming from. I hadn't grown up being stopped and searched, or being made fun of at school for my name. Sure, I'd had some experiences of my own: I'd been followed around beauty shops by Asian shopkeepers; I'd left a pub in the Cotswolds because of hostile stares from other patrons and being ignored by the bar staff. These experiences were trivial, but I understood how a lifetime of such microaggressions might shape my view of the world. I began to appreciate the privilege of growing up in a country where I had been the norm. Being in a system like that during my formative years had cloaked me in self-confidence.

But the longer I lived in Britain, the more I started to notice a few things about myself that I had previously been blind to.

When I met up with a friend I hadn't seen in years, I noticed she had gone natural. 'Why not?' she'd said, when I asked her why. The last time I'd seen my hair in its natural state, I was 11. Adult black women did not have natural hair. We had braids. We had weaves. We had wigs. At the very least, we had relaxed hair. Why was that?

In my job I was working with a number of Europeans, mostly Spaniards and Italians. Many of them spoke broken English and thought nothing of it. Why would they speak English properly when it wasn't their native tongue? My mother tongue is Yoruba but English is my first language. I think in English. My parents never taught me or my siblings Yoruba. They spoke the language to each other but never to us. There was the prevailing belief that if they taught us Yoruba first, our English would be tainted. The grasp of English was not only shorthand for class but also for intelligence. They thought we'd pick up Yoruba by osmosis, but 'vernacular' wasn't permitted in schools. Why was that?

And then I read Frantz Fanon's *Black Skin, White Masks*, a devastating analysis of the effect of colonial domination on the human psyche. The book was published nearly seventy years ago but I saw myself in its pages. For the first time I understood why the first short story I'd ever written had included no black characters. I understood why I was fascinated with Greek mythology but believed that the pantheon of Yoruba gods were evil and forbidden.

Psychologists and neuroscientists tell us that the unconscious – a sophisticated yet hidden set of mental processes – is responsible for the majority of our judgements, feelings and actions. Could it be that growing up in Nigeria, while it empowered me with the self-confidence to navigate the western world, had also buried a self-hate so deep in me, I didn't even know it existed? And how had that shaped my view of the world and my place within it?

So, I shaved off all my hair.

It was symbolic of a new beginning, my decision to seek out all the areas of my life where I might have internalised inferiority and begin to unlearn it. It was also an acknowledgement, a sign to those around me that I was now treading the path to self-knowledge. I watched my hair grow out of my head just as it was meant to. Some days I'd hate the way I looked and overcompensate with too much makeup and jewellery. Other days I couldn't stop twirling my curls around my finger. In time, I wondered why I'd ever spent so much time, money and energy trying to look like someone else. Now I wear my afro tall, proud and picked to the gods.

I started to learn about Yoruba religion and the orisas. I will never practise Yoruba religion but I'm learning to uncouple it from the heavy demonisation and enjoy the tales for what they are – an alternate interpretation of the world, the values my ancestors sought to pass down to me.

People say not everything is about self-hate, sometimes it's just preference. Maybe that's true but I might have lived an entire lifetime in Nigeria thinking I preferred my hair straight. I might have never confronted all the reasons why the mere mention of Yoruba religion made me feel scared. I might have continued to feel privileged for growing up in Nigeria, without confronting the deeply rooted beliefs that were reinforced by the system and everyone around me. Harmful beliefs baked into the psyche of a nation hastily created by the British Empire.

I had to move to Britain to find and embrace my true self.

CANDICE BRATHWAITE

We first met Candice at a brunch in celebration of the publication of our companion to the original *Slay In Your Lane* book, *Slay In Your Lane: The Journal,* and became even bigger fans of the 'Mummy Blogger' and founder of Make Motherhood Diverse – an online initiative that aims to encourage a more accurately representative and diverse depiction of motherhood in the media. This is something Candice does through the documentation of her own experiences as a black mother on her Instagram account and the release of her debut book *I Am Not Your Baby Mother.* Her essay focuses on the idea that children should be 'seen and not heard', a mantra she has had to challenge and unlearn since becoming a mother.

To Be Seen and Heard,
That's Where Power Is . . .

I'm raising a brave little black girl.

So brave that one day she did something perhaps no woman or man has dared to do before.

Let me explain.

I, her mother, am from a liberal Caribbean background. One-part Bajan and the other Jamaican, I of course believe that on some occasions it is necessary to be strict. But while I am raising a well-mannered, disciplined child, I try to keep my eyes, heart and mind open. I was raised in a unique setting, which I will tell you about in a moment, in which, while there were obvious parameters of obedience, the door was always open for me to discuss how I was feeling.

My daughter's father could not have been raised in a more different household. He was born and raised in Nigeria and then migrated to the UK in his early teens; he grew up in a space ruled more by fear than by actual respect (many seem to confuse the latter for the former) and made sure to make himself disappear once his father came home. We have traded stories of our upbringing and together we seem to have struck a balance in our parenting that works for us. I have picked out the parts of his childhood which I think will help my children develop into responsible adults and he has taken the softness that I experienced and sought to make it his own. Between us we're raising a six-year-old daughter and an almost two-year-old son in a manner that *respectfully* encourages them to use their voices. And one afternoon we were unexpectedly given front-row seats to the very example of what we are trying to encourage in our children.

My father-in-law was in town, and when he is, he likes to spend the bulk of his time visiting his grandchildren. We get along fine, very well in fact. While I'm sure that my independent woman vibes were discombobulating to him at first, he soon recognised that ultimately his son loved me, and so there are some things I assume he is willing to overlook.

That particular afternoon, having just eaten lunch, he asked my daughter Esmé to please take his plate into the kitchen.

'But Grandpa, why?' she asked. She assessed him. 'There is nothing wrong with your legs.'

Her father and I were in the kitchen at the time, and we paused. But the reasons for the momentary holding of our breaths were different.

'I know there is nothing wrong with my legs but it is about respect. If I ask you to take my plate to the kitchen, you should take it,' he began to explain. 'Where I am from, if I ask a younger person to do something for me, they do it without asking questions. That is respect.'

There was a moment of silence, which I knew Esmé was using to craft her comeback.

'Well no, I respect my Nana but she never asks me to clear her plate. And sometimes,' she added, 'she needs to use a walking stick.' She was trying to drive the point home that her grandfather seemed to be lacking a disability, which might stop him from taking the plate himself.

'But I'm not talking about your Nana. I am your Grandpa and I expect you take my plate,' he shot back.

'Listen,' I whispered to my husband (more commonly and affectionately known as Papa B), 'you better get in there, cause if it has to be me . . .' I tipped my head and raised my eyebrows, giving the universal black woman look that is usually translated as 'Someone is gonna know what time it is.'

And that someone wasn't going to be my daughter.

Many might argue that I should've known what kind of culture I was choosing to marry into. And indeed, when I later recounted the story on Instagram, there were some women who were flat-out mortified that I didn't expect Esmé to take her grandfather's plate. Some even went on to ask in outraged tones, what would happen if my daughter were to give the same response to a future husband who might ask her to do the same thing? (Assuming she would be in a relationship with a man.) And finally, and I think this was the response that made me saddest of all, some women actually tagged men asking them for their reactions to this disrespect – in part proving my point that there was no way I was going to let Esmé pick up that plate in the first place.

When it comes to the black community, it feels as though women are constantly expected to be in service to others, but most notably to other *men*. Our social media feeds are filled with unnecessary advice about what black women should be doing to 'catch' and 'keep' a man. But there is very little offered up to black boys and men about what they could perhaps be doing for a woman to *want* to catch and keep them in the first place. All our relationship conversations seem to be geared towards learning how to please men, with very little consideration given to what this might do to both our mental and physical health. We are completely disrespected by the world, but are still expected to hold it up. When I speak to people about our society, I often use a pyramid to help illustrate my point. At the top of the pyramid are white men. Just below them comes white women, and after that it's men and women of any other race except black. The final slab of the pyramid belongs to black men. And black women? We don't even get gifted a space on the pyramid. We are the pillars, entrenched by the soil, holding the pyramid aloft but never given the chance to be seen, let alone heard.

So whilst on the surface, her grandfather's request might have appeared simple, for me, knowing what I want for my daughter, it was rooted in something far deeper. Would he have asked the same of my son? He is completely able bodied, so why could he not walk to the kitchen, which was less than ten paces away? Was this about respect or was it about the expectation, for young girls especially, to be submissive and silent?

This is not how I was raised.

In *my* childhood, whilst my mother and nan went out to work, I was raised by my maternal grandfather. A violent mugging had left him blind in one eye and he was deemed unfit for work. Without hesitation he stepped into the role of caregiver and homemaker, never missing a beat when it came to ironing my school uniform or using the skills he had acquired as a head chef to prepare delicious and nutritious meals for the entire family. It was not until I had children of my own that I began to meditate on what that experience must have been like for him. If he ever felt as though his masculinity had been diminished by taking up the role usually associated with women, he never showed it. As well as demonstrating to me that men could, and should, do domestic work he encouraged me to be independent and use my voice. He reiterated the importance of a woman being able to speak and act for herself, offering up quite mature examples, like the O. J. Simpson trial (which he encouraged me to follow even at such a young age), in order to give me space to form my own opinion and pick sense out of nonsense.

When my Nan would try to send me upstairs, declaring that 'children should be seen and not heard' my Grandad would not allow it. 'Why hide the truth from her? Better she learn from us than from those on the streets.'

But as I grew up, I began to clock how unique his way of thinking was and just how tightly the black community clung to a mindset similar to my Nan's, irrespective of the impact of such beliefs. Because what I also learned is that being seen and not heard usually leads to feelings of inadequacy, or the sense that even if we did speak up about something wrong happening around or to us, we are unlikely to be believed. To be constantly hushed and shooed away as a child means that the skills required to stand up and speak out as an adult just aren't going to be there.

I have witnessed the effects of this on many black women in adulthood. Sometimes it leaves them feeling unable to ask for a promotion at work. But there are many more extreme, and sometimes horrific, examples. This was made clear to me in a video that went viral a few years before the #MeToo movement. In it, a young black woman (seemingly in her early to mid-twenties) was at a family gathering at which she confronted a family member who had sexually assaulted her. What pained me the most was to see that no one appeared shocked or even the least bothered by her accusation. It seemed like no one believed her. And where did that habit of not being believed originate? It had to be from always being made to feel that her voice was not worthy in the first place. It seems to me that a veil of secrecy, having your voice muted and constantly being told that you don't even have the right to question something, has a lot to do with it.

My Grandad's support of the use of my voice is, in part, why I have the career I do. In a space where I see far too few reflections of myself it can be easy to be overwhelmed into silence, as I'm scared of what speaking up and out could do to my career and therefore my bag. But whenever I feel unsure, I remember how much better I felt when he encouraged me to challenge something or at the very least to have an opinion. And in doing so, I think radiating such energy has allowed me to attract a man who is very much like my Grandad.

Papa B is a man who doesn't care for the societal pressures that help determine a man's masculinity. I can perhaps count on one hand the amount of times I have cooked for him ('I keep sweaters in my stove,' as Carrie Bradshaw once said); when it comes to the children he has more patience than I could pray for and he prefers to clean the bathroom taps, because apparently bathroom cleaner and Vikal aren't the same thing. Household chores aside, he encourages me to speak up in the same manner that my Grandad did, subconsciously encouraging our daughter to do the same thing.

'I have seen what happens to a woman when she feels disempowered and silenced. If there is any way that I can help reverse some of that trauma, I'm all for it,' he admitted one day.

Having been raised in a space and society which, perhaps up until this very day, prefers to listen to men rather than women, I sometimes wonder if he understands how powerful this is. That particular afternoon, he went into the living room and supported Esmé's choice.

'Dad, I know this will be hard for you to understand but this isn't how we do things here. Esmé doesn't take our plates. She is polite and helpful, but that just isn't something we expect from her.' He spoke firmly.

'Man, I don't know for your this UK. In my eyes it is simply an issue of respect, that's all.'

I felt the grip on the plate I was holding grow tight. My daughter was one of the most respectful children I knew and for it to even be suggested that she could be anything but made my blood pressure rise.

'I'll take the plate,' Bodé confirmed with a tone that suggested he would hear no more about it.

The living room fell silent and all that could be heard was the soft clinking of cutlery.

It annoyed me, because to this very day, my own Grandad would never expect me to take his plate. In fact, whenever I've been blessed enough to be fed by him, he hovers in an almost annoying manner, constantly enquiring if there is anything he can get me to make the experience better. And I've never thought of him as a servant or a skivvy, but instead as someone who takes his role as caregiver very seriously, yet still gets all of my love and respect. In showing me that it is ok to speak up, he, in a plethora of ways, set an example for me. It means that whatever situation arises, I'm always very aware of who has the power in the room, and I communicate with them based on the amount of courtesy needed for their position at the time – because that's how you can get your point across respectfully.

So, my hope is that, in some small way the community I adore starts to understand how important it is to allow the younger generations to be seen *and* heard should the situation call for it. Whenever a question isn't met with an immediate act of servitude, or a 'yes' this shouldn't always be interpreted as a total disregard for authority. Instead it should offer a time and space for us to ask why that child's intuition might have made them feel affronted in the first place. It's important to remember that silencing is a tool often used in situations likened to enslavement and imprisonment, and shutting a child down before they've even had a chance to communicate should not be our default parenting tool, especially in a community that is still dealing with the personal and public fallout of being silenced as an entire race.

After that day, Bodé and I didn't spend much time meditating on the situation, because we both agreed that Esmé didn't have to take her grandfather's plate. But I still understood that there were some things rooted within his culture that I couldn't make it my duty to dismantle. Not every big change needs to begin with a fanfare. I have seen the power of small ripples and how over time they can lead to a tsunami, which changes the landscape of a culture forever. This isn't to say that we know it all or that our daughter is perfect, but the choice that we made in that moment, felt right for us. And a few weeks later her actions confirmed it.

It was late in the evening and I had made the rare decision to eat dinner in front of the television. Once I had finished, I set my plate aside and didn't give it much more thought.

'Mummy have you finished your dinner?' Esmé asked sweetly.

'Yeah babe I'm stuffed,' I responded

'Would you like me to take your plate to the kitchen?' she asked, without agenda.

I paused, looking at her with a pride which can only be felt when a parent is able to see that their child completely understands something, which in many ways can never be explained. And by the time I came to myself and was able to respond, I heard the soft clink of my plate hitting the kitchen sink. She hadn't even bothered to wait for my response, she had taken the plate anyway and in that quick moment I was reminded that there will always be power in allowing a child to be seen and heard.

CHARLIE BRINKHURST-CUFF

We have worked with Charlie several times and there's no one in the industry whose continued levelling is more inspiring to witness. She is an award-winning writer, editor and columnist, and Head of Editorial at *gal-dem* magazine. She also curated the timely and important anthology *Mother Country: Real Stories of the Windrush Children* in 2018, using the Windrush scandal as a starting point to explore the rich and varied stories of British Caribbeans. In her essay, she writes with her usual eloquence about navigating a world where black women are often characterised as 'loud', when you're a 'shy black girl'.

How I Learned to be a
Shy Loud Black Girl

My shyness is bitter and inconsistent. It is the type of shyness that rolls up my tongue and heats my face and makes me shake. When I was younger, I viewed it almost as another entity from myself. It wasn't me. It was a frustrating something-or-other being which crept into my life at the times when I wanted to take opportunities and snatched them away from me. It would put up a thick, invisible barrier between me and my understanding of heaven. A place where I could talk to anyone, express myself and never be silenced.

Early on in life my own battle against shyness was complicated by the fact that black British girls don't really get to be shy. Pop culture expectations of loudness, brashness and confidence are often folded into the fizzing mixture of our upbringings. Growing up, especially in white environments like so many of us do – in the 2011 census, making up only 3 per cent of the UK's population[1] – our friends might expect us to be able to twerk for them or rap all the lyrics to Ray BLK's latest track in front of a crowd. At best we are playfully viewed as performers. At worst, our blackness is used to stereotype our innocent behaviours and teachers or other authority figures deem us 'rude' or 'disinterested' because of facial expressions or actions predicated by our shyness.

At school I was once made to sing a duet with a boy, 'Baby It's Cold Outside', for the Christmas concert. Even though I blushed every time I had to hold my partner's hand, and cringed at this white boy's attempt at scat singing, even though I kept messing up the harmony at the end, the optics of having a young black girl singing that soulful (if slightly rapey) song, obviously looked good for the school. Before we went on stage, I imagined the laughter of the parents. I was too embarrassed to invite my own family. On another occasion, I was pulled into a nasty interaction with a teacher who told me that just because I was black, that didn't mean I could get away with giving him dirty looks and that I didn't engage enough in class. Funnily enough, I still got an A in the externally marked exam for his subject.

Shyness is a national condition. In the UK, a 2019 survey conducted by YouGov and *The Times* found that 47 per cent of British adults regard themselves as shy.[2] Of course, there is no real consensus on what qualifies someone as being shy, other than it being a feeling of nervousness around others. Despite this, 'shyness' can slip into the diagnosable definitions of social anxiety with ease – fearing criticism, avoiding eye contact, dreading interactions with strangers, panic attacks and palpitations are all things I've experienced without meeting the criteria of having a social phobia.[3] I'm sure many people have felt inconsistent shyness, would describe themselves as shy even though all outward appearances would prove otherwise, would say shyness such as what I have described is not shyness at all, or conflate shyness and social anxiety to higher degree than I have here. I accept that self-diagnosis of shyness is flawed, that there will always be someone who feels it more than I do.

But I also refuse to deny my own experiences and the experiences of my peers. Black girls, as studies have shown, are viewed as much older than white girls. They are sexualised and seen as 'less innocent' to the degree that, as I have found during interviews,[4] they are catcalled from when they are young children, and followed around stores. In the case of eighteen-year-old Jay Belnavis-McPherson, they have their heads slammed into dirty ground at London Bridge station by the police, breaking their teeth, for 'smelling of weed';[5] or, in the case of twenty-year-old Joy Morgan, they are not seen as innocent or deserving enough of press coverage after they go missing.[6] Not even after it has been found that they have been murdered.

If confidence comes with age and most of us leave our shyness behind with our baby teeth, it is not a reach to link the way in which we are perceived to be older than our age, to the way in which we are perceived to be louder and less shy than our peers of different races. The problem is that when you deal a hand of cards in sickly stereotypes, there will always be black girls who are left behind. In the US, they are calling it 'adultification bias'.[7]

One of the first real memories I have of being shy was on my first day of primary school. London, Hackney, 1998. I am five and a bit. I have started school later than my peers – both in terms of it no longer being the start of September, and on this day it not being 8 a.m. My dad and I are late for school. I've shuffled into a small, white and yellow-rimmed classroom stuffed with too many desks and thin, curling alphabet letters on the whiteboard. It's time for my dad to go. He can't leave though. He's dressed in a massive green trench coat, which stretches down almost to his ankles and has a thick lining – there is plenty of space for me to hide. In front of all of my new classmates, I cower into the folds of his coat. I can't remember if I was clutching his leg. My memory ends there.

Those first few years of school were no fun though. Really, I only had one friend, Alice, and then briefly another friend, Luca, who came and went in a puff of Italian intrigue for a single school year. They are the only two people I remember having conversations with at school. Even now, I treasure the memory of those friendships deeply. Alice, Luca and a friend I made called Maria-Daniella were pretty much the only people I connected with outside of family friendships between the ages of five and eight. Over the years I've looked for them all, tracked them down on Facebook and other forms of social media. Last I heard, Alice was a flourishing graduate and Luca was an excellent musician, but I didn't ever find Maria-Daniella, who had a fantastic collection of delicate Russian dancer Barbie dolls and a sweet smile. She especially was so important to me because, unlike with the rest of the world, I could talk to her freely. Everyone else, I was a little afraid of.

As I moved up in the years at primary school, and then high school, I began to watch the confident girls closely. The way they spoke and articulated would never be something I could emulate. I couldn't be soft, cute, funny and magnetic just by being me, because I wasn't white enough. I wasn't self-assured enough. I felt pressure to lean into some of the stereotypes of my race, and I hadn't been educated well enough in the realm of blackness to know that I didn't have to do this. I sexualised myself in uncomfortable ways, wore push-up bras as thick as the socks the previous generation used to stuff, was desperate to lose my virginity and saw it as a stain on my character that I didn't have the confidence to do so. I let boys tell me they were 'into black girls' while they kissed my neck and practically sought out situations to be dehumanised.

What I have realised, is that black women's shyness once they're all grown up is so unusual that it becomes a spectacle. Take the American singer, Summer Walker. Her shyness and introversion (in·tro·vert 1. a shy, reticent person), of course, falls into that diagnosable realm of social anxiety. In 2019, the then 23-year-old cancelled more than half of her remaining US tour, twenty gigs, because she was struggling with the process. 'I'm not going to be able to finish this tour because it doesn't really coexist with my social anxiety and my introverted personality,' she wrote on Instagram. 'I'm a person, I have feelings. I get tired, I get sad and it's just a lot.'

But Summer wasn't allowed to just *be* with her gorgeous, buttery vocals. The narrative and believability of her social anxiety and shyness were dragged through the mud of popular discourse.

She was deemed a 'faker', told she should learn to just deal with the pressures of fame. Back on Instagram she stuck up for herself, saying that, 'You know the scariest shit I've been witnessing is that most of the women leaving negative comments like "it's an act", "I don't have the right to act like this b/c I'm famous", "bitch you slow" or just flat out making fun of me for being vulnerable.' There are a plethora of white women singers out there presenting as introverted; it very much could be misogynoir that has laid Walker out to dry, made her an anomaly, a spectacle, because people across the races struggle with black performers who don't conform to a Beyoncé standard of in-your-face entertainment.

The lens of racism is complex, though. For me, overt racism in high school aimed at me and at others meant I had to learn to be loud in the most uncomfortable of situations because I quickly realised that few others would do it for me. I needed to be able to bite back against injustice and racism when I heard and saw it. But in the later years of school I was immensely upset when my friends started to make fun of the fact that I would speak up. 'Don't say that around Charlie, she'll get angry with you,' was a common epithet. It made me want to stop speaking up, to recede into that shyness, and at times I did. I shrunk myself and pretended I wasn't bothered by ignorant humour because, I argued internally, I didn't want people to feel like I was a killjoy, and also it felt better to know their true opinions on things.

I still battle with this today, except in my writing. This is the space where I feel I can be persuasive and bold and challenging. Where I can reflect, learn and inspire. My natural state teeters between anxiety and bravery, a light depression and happiness I believe will be tainted momentarily. I am frustrated that I had to learn to be loud in the way that I did. Sometimes I think that maybe I should recede back into shyness and become a quiet academic who studies and tries to reason people out of their prejudices with all the knowledge that I'm not quite afforded the time and space to explore as a full-time journalist. I didn't have a choice in becoming a 'commentator' because my opinion was sought very early on in my career. I always knew I had a lot of catching up to do.

Looking back, I believe that my shyness as a black girl was not allowed to develop into a quiet confidence, or a 'loudness', in the 'normal' way. We are forced out of comfort zones from early on. Naturally, I was fighting my shyness too. In my own careful way I was trying to learn how to be less anxious, afraid of the world, afraid of talking to boys and making friends with girls and everything else that comes along with being a teenager. I'm not saying that we shouldn't all be trying to be more confident. It feels good now, to have learnt – to some degree – how to speak up. And studies have consistently found that confident people are happier.[8] The point is that this should be on our own terms.

References

1 '2011 Census analysis: Ethnicity and religion of the non-UK born population in England and Wales: 2011', Office for National Statistics, (18 June 2015) <https://www.ons.gov.uk/peoplepopulationand community/culturalidentity/ethnicity/articles/2011censusanalysis ethnicityandreligionofthenonuk bornpopulationinenglandandwales/ 2015-06-18>

2 Greg Hurst, 'More than half of Britons secretly admit they are shy', *The Times*, (11 November 2019) <https://www.thetimes.co.uk/article/ more-than-half-of-britons-secretly-admit-they-are-shy-379vl66sr>

3 'Shyness and social phobia', Royal College of Psychiatrists, <https:// www.rcpsych.ac.uk/mental-health/problems-disorders/shyness-and-social-phobia>

4 Charlie Brinkhurst-Cuff, 'Less innocent, more adult: the unfair perceptions that haunt young black girls', *Guardian*, (24 October 2017) <https://www.theguardian.com/inequality/2017/oct/24/less-innocent-more-adult-the-unfair-perceptions-that-haunt-young-black-girls>

5 Neelam Tailor, 'This week a London police break a black girl's tooth and the UK sees its first black woman history professor', *gal-dem*, (4 November 2019) <http://gal-dem.com/race-review-a-black-girl-was-attacked-by-london-police-and-the-uk-sees-its-first-black-woman-history-professor/>

6 Charlie Brinkhurst-Cuff, 'Joy Morgan can be laid to rest, but more needs to be uncovered about her murder', *gal-dem*, (11 October 2019) <http://gal-dem.com/joy-morgan-can-be-laid-to-rest-but-more-needs-to-be-uncovered-about-her-murder/>

7 'Research Confirms that Black Girls Feel the Sting of Adultification Bias Identified in Earlier Georgetown Law Study', Georgetown Law, (15 May 2019) <https://www.law.georgetown.edu/news/research-confirms-that-black-girls-feel-the-sting-of-adultification-bias-identified-in-earlier-georgetown-law-study/>

8 Evelyn Marinoff, 'Confident People Found Happiest in the World', *Evelyn Marinoff* [blog], (28 January 2018) <http://www.evelyn marinoff.com/confident-people-found-happiest-people-world/>

ELISABETH FAPURO

When we set out to curate this anthology it was really important to us to feature an emerging talent, found through an open submission competition. We want to continue to empower and inspire others to write about whatever is relevant to them as a black woman today and to celebrate their own stories. We were blown away by how exciting, bright and brilliant the many essays submitted were, and it was a pleasure to read every single one.

Sadly, we could only pick one winner. But we are so proud to announce the winner: Elisabeth Fapuro, a 2014 Literature graduate and Future Trainee at an international US law firm. Her essay stood out as a great way to critically explore our relationship with Black Excellence. We particularly love the way that Elisabeth delivers her argument in a way that is educational, relatable and often very funny.

The 'Shuri' Effect:
The Age of #Blackexcellence,
the Falsehood of Black Mediocrity
and the Absence of the
Black Middle

The talking drums started and the depth of their calling fortified me. Their message was unexpected, unfamiliar but welcome, and it called to an audience who for too long had been ignored.

It was February 2018 and I was sitting in an all-black, all-female screening of *Black Panther* at Stratford Picturehouse with my favourites at the BlackGirlsBookClub. The uniqueness of the experience – being part of a sold-out black female screening of a Hollywood film with a predominantly black cast – made it quasi-spiritual. Since its release *Black Panther* has gone on to achieve several deserved accolades including highest-grossing solo superhero film, highest-grossing film by a black director and highest opening weekend gross for a predominantly black cast. A film that proudly shatters negative stereotypes by depicting an economically thriving, independent and scientifically advanced African nation. Perhaps singularly embodied in the Wakandan princess-cum-genius Shuri – played by our good sis Letitia Wright. It was in essence the epitome of 'Black Excellence'. Yes, Black Excellence, that ship which, if you're a black Briton like me who struggles with feelings of mediocrity, you feel like passed you by at a distance with every Femi and Tunde aboard. Black

Excellence makes me feel how I imagine those of you who missed *Afronation* must have felt watching our Instagram stories. But you're not going crazy, the concept of Black Excellence whilst an unapologetic rejection of the narrative that blackness cannot be brilliant, is complex in the sense that it also risks alienating black individuals who believe they cannot achieve the required standard of 'excellence'. A standard often not required of our white counterparts. Before we take a look at this it is necessary to take a look at what #blackexcellence is a reaction against.

Shuri: separating intelligence and excellence from whiteness

In modern society there has been a standardised association of intelligence with whiteness. Within the context of so-called 'race theory', the idea of there being a genetic difference between the races, reflecting itself in an intelligence gap is an alluring 'justification for bigotry and racial inequality'.[1] As a result, the greater a black individual's intelligence, the greater their perceived proximity to whiteness. In mainstream media, so-called 'blerds' (black nerds) and bleeks (black geeks) including the Carlton Bankses and Steve Urkels were positioned closer to stereotypes associated with whiteness, by virtue of their intelligence. Not cool *enough* to be black, and *too* smart to be black. You know – *black*, black. Thinking back to my own childhood, being a classically trained violinist who performed well at school and was well spoken automatically narrowed my distance to whiteness in the minds of my peers. This perception carried with it the occasional call for me to 'stop acting white'. Shuri embodied the rejection of this narrative, by virtue of her ingenuity and brilliance being nurtured and centred in Wakanda. In Africa. In blackness. No western education in sight, Ryan Coogler allowed Shuri's excellence to be portrayed as a direct *result* of her blackness. To call this portrayal 'refreshing' does not seem to pay Coogler enough credit for what in mainstream terms was a bold move.

Of course, for many of us across the diaspora, the Shuri figure is nothing new. Black people have been overachieving intellectually for centuries. Yes, even *outside* of Egypt. From the great lost libraries and manuscripts of Timbuktu, whose university was founded around the same time as Oxford,[2] to the ancient Nigerian script *Nsibidi*, independent of Roman, Latin or Arabic influence, which dates back to 2000 BC[3] and provided the inspiration for symbolism used in *Black Panther*.[4] And our intelligence shouldn't be defined in historical terms, as our good brother Ramarni Wilfred from east London shows, who at sixteen has an IQ higher than Bill Gates and the estimated 160 of Einstein.[5]

Strategically, the notion of the 'civilising mission' was used as the rationale for the western colonisation of various black and ethnic populations from the fifteenth to the twentieth century.[6] In order to morally justify the purely economic motives for intervention, colonisation had to be premised on the idea that black people were intellectually inferior to their white counterparts. The combined effect of imperialism, colonialism and the transatlantic slave trade on the black consciousness, therefore, was to perpetuate the idea that black achievement is anomalous. This was done through highly unimaginative means including the removal of black people from their land to try and suppress their knowledge of their culture and history, creating a global mainstream media designed to focus on white achievement and building global economic and educational structures centred around whiteness. In the UK educational system, despite the utilisation of a whitewashed global history which ignores black social identity and contribution (apart from slavery of course let's focus on the time they were enslaved) black pupils are still achieving, yet less likely to be admitted into university despite equivalent A-level results.[7] This distancing of blackness and intelligence hurts black individuals attempting to enter the UK's most prestigious educational institutions like Oxford as they are disproportionately more likely to be mis-predicted grades[8] which in itself shows they are more often perceived as less capable by their teachers. The dichotomy however is twofold, as for the black consciousness to surrender to its supposed inferiority through this conditioning, the same conditioning must infiltrate the white consciousness into believing its superiority.

So despite having cultivated some of the greatest civilisations in history, the Black Excellence movement is positioned as relatively new in social media standards. When utilised within the community the term can be a powerful means of amplifying the achievements of black individuals who go on to achieve despite the prejudices and institutional racism they encounter. However, the corresponding societal reaction seems to have been a sudden 'realisation' of the potential of black individuals to *be* excellent. In the corporate space, the resulting response has been a mass emergence of widespread Diversity and Inclusion or D&I programmes (read: D very much *without* the I) that pride themselves on 'progressively' diversifying their business by 'allowing' the 'best' black candidates to occupy their spaces without a thought to changing the exclusionary cultures which dismissed them in the first place. This commodification of Black Excellence is used to forgive the past and present discriminatory recruiting practices by British employers (which still continue to disadvantage black applicants) by perpetuating the narrative that not hiring any black people before was fine because they are now able to attract the 'best black' talent which just wasn't there before. This narrative minimises unconscious bias (read: very conscious-unconscious bias) as a factor for previous practices, in preference of the more digestible falsehood that there has been an emergence of a more able black workforce.

The implication that before the rise of Black Excellence, black people and their contribution to British society was defined by its inferiority is harmful. The talent was always there.

At this point, it's worth clarifying that in a society that is defined by perpetuating negative stereotypes of black individuals – from the angry black woman, to Kentucky-fried-knife-crime[9] – I celebrate black achievement at every point. However, the only way to dispel generation-long anti-black stereotypes that exist in mainstream media should not be by being judged to a standard far greater than that our non-black counterparts are expected to reach. This risks cultivating the notion that black individuals are only worthy of being noticed, of recognition, if we meet the standard of exceptionalism, of 'excellence'.

The 'best black' complex

The narrative that many of us second generation black Britons were raised on was that in order to succeed in white spaces we needed to be the 'best black'. To be fair on our parents, this was less geared towards embedding a fear of failure into our psyche, and more of an attempt by them to vicariously eradicate the educational and professional barriers that defined their own working lives. Rather too simplistically, we were raised on the idea that the greater our educational success, the greater the chance of our upward social mobility. This of course is true, however greater earning power (read: flashier corporate job) does not equate to less discrimination. Our parents optimistically premised this approach on the basis that the next generation of black Britons would not face the same overt discrimination in the workplace as they had. Again, they were right. We've passed the overt widespread racism that emboldened employers to exclude 'coloureds' from applying to vacancies prior to the 1968 Race Relations Act, and have transitioned to a form of discrimination far more insidious. It is in fact quite *British* in its 'politeness', and operates before black individuals even enter the workplace.

A study by the Centre for Social Investigation at Nuffield College, University of Oxford, found that minority ethnic applicants had to send 80 per cent more applications to get a positive response from an employer than a white person of British origin.[10] Once results were compared with similar field experiments dating back to 1969, it revealed that discrimination against black Britons and those of south Asian origin were unchanged over almost fifty years. Quite remarkable, seeing as the majority of British society will have you believe that they just 'can't believe that racism still exists . . . in 2020'. As if moving further into the future moves us further away from the 'bad years' which can be isolated as the period where black individuals were treated 'badly'. Or the 'I don't see race' proponents who utilise the statement as a means of silencing black peoples' legitimate experiences concerning their blackness. The results show that ethnic minority applicants are often not shortlisted on the basis of their ethnicity, particularly prejudicing those with 'ethnic' sounding names. *Eighty per cent.* Eighty per cent more applications, 80 per cent more time spent wrongly contemplating our false sense of inferiority due to factors beyond our control.

The results of studies like these qualify a statement a good friend of mine once made: all black people are inherently working class by virtue of their blackness. For many of our parents this was a reality, often coming from overseas as highly skilled workers and being forced into lower skilled, lower paid jobs due to a system which often did not recognise the validity of their overseas qualifications. A system that also coaxed our parents into believing they were inferior. For us millennials (and later generations) the premise is less literal, but true all the same. Despite our professional and academic achievements, the visual impact of our blackness in corporate spaces bears with it a plethora of false assumptions that aim to delegitimise our right to occupy our spaces in those environments. That we are *less* able than our white counterparts. That we are *less* capable of articulating ourselves. That we are undeserving of being paid equally to our white counterparts, despite studies showing that a more diverse workforce translates into greater profitability for our employers.[11][12]

For the white corporate status quo, the best black complex is the ultimate desired effect of these pre-application biases, their delegitimisation of our right to occupy corporate spaces and other anti-black prejudices. The best black complex is the material-isation of a Darwinian 'survival of the fittest' mode that black people develop in corporate spaces, which falsely encourages us to believe that *only* other black individuals are our competitors. Why? Because white mediocrity does not exist: societal struc-tures does not allow *whiteness* to be mediocre. As a result, black individuals are not given the opportunity to 'compete' with their white counterparts in working environments and are instead deliberately measured against other BAME (read: black) candi-dates. This in turn fractures our sense of community within the very (white) working environments where we need solidarity the most. It is the initial joy once we see another black candidate at an interview that turns into a realisation that we are likely being pitted against each other to occupy the one space allocated for the 'diverse' candidate on the intake, despite whether we validate our spaces as the strongest candidates. In this way black individuals often navigate what I've come to term a 'hyper(in)visibility' in corporate spaces. The 'hyper' visibility of our blackness, or differ-ence, that causes employers to act out their prejudices against us in the form of microaggressions, juxtaposed with the lack of value placed on our 'invisible' contribution in work environ-ments.

The complexity in the discussion lies here. Arguably, Black Excellence in its 'purest' form seeks to shifts the diaspora towards forming a community in our brilliance and away from 'best black' complexes that centre our brilliance on divisive terms (i.e. for one black candidate to succeed, the others must fail). So what's the problem then? The problem lies in 'the middle'.

The absence of the 'middle'

Criticisms of Black Excellence should not be interpreted as a rallying cry for black individuals to limit themselves to 'mediocrity'. Rather, they are a recognition of the fact that our lack of equality in society often stems from us not being allowed to occupy 'the middle'.

> Mediocre (*adj.*) . . . from Latin mediocris 'of middling height or state, moderate, ordinary,' . . . from medius '**middle**'[13]

In mainstream media, black individuals are mostly depicted as extreme examples on either end of the spectrum. Whether it's the aforementioned Carlton Banks or Steve Urkel-esque nerds or the drug-dealing James St Patricks of the world.[14] As black women in particular we are both the hyper-sexualised 'Jezebel' and the desexualised 'Mammy',[15] often never progressing beyond the 'white-female-romantic-lead's-best-friend' role. In the case of the 'Mammy' stereotype, this desexualisation on screen translates into real life perceptions of black women as revealed by a 2014 *OkCupid* poll on race and attraction which showed that black women were perceived as the least desirable romantic partner among all racial groups.[16] These polarising depictions echo the outskirts of society we are confined to in everyday life: geographically, socially and economically. We are never granted the privilege of the average in mainstream media. The average law-abiding black citizen who doesn't carry a knife or engage in gun violence. The average modern black millennial who goes on to complete university and work in the city alongside their white peers. The average black girl who minds her business and isn't irrationally angry like the media would have you believe (I'm not an angry black girl, but I am however a 'Loud Black Girl').

It's important here for me to draw a distinction between 'black mediocrity', the unfounded negative stereotype historically perpetuated by white societal structures to impose limitations on black people (which I refer to in the title of my essay), and the ability of black people as individuals to occupy the middle and engage in mediocrity without the consistent pressure of rising to excellence in their everyday lives.

The result of stereotypes like these is that the black individuals who subvert these narratives are hailed as exceptions by mainstream media who then look to them as 'authorities of blackness'. Whilst within the black community we realise and appreciate the heterogeneity of our existence, wider society isn't as allowing of the diversity of our thought to be broadcast. These 'exceptions' are then called upon to define a singular black opinion on any given issue affecting the black community. Black Excellence then risks becoming performative, where the same black voices are asked to articulate intersectional aspects of the black experience they cannot identify with. Occasionally, the media's motives here can be in giving a voice to those black individuals most predisposed to co-sign their agenda. A good example here is the *Good Morning Britain* segment regarding the Stacey Dooley 'white saviour' row, where the inclusion of black journalist Ed Adoo (who vehemently defended Stacey's intentions) seemed to be purely for the purposes of delegitimising another black voice, in this case David Lammy.[17][18] Essentially, this was whiteness giving a platform to one black voice, to silence another black voice. Of course, it is a problem in itself that as black people when we vocalise our individual perspectives, it is seen as representative of a homogenous black experience. This relates again to the idea of hyper(in)visibility where black individuals are seen as a hyper-visible, indivisible collective (the 'other') and individuality is reserved as a privilege of whiteness. This being the case, in order to change the narrative we need to be able to mobilise the voices within our community which not only highlight the diversity of our thought and experience, but also the intersectionality of our diversity.

I started writing this piece from a place of frustration. Working within the corporate legal sector, it was a frustration that by virtue of my under representation, I had unwillingly consented to amplifying this standard of 'Black Excellence' that just didn't seem sustainable in everyday life. In writing this piece I sought to perhaps revolt against Black Excellence as a concept, but in deconstructing it found nuance.

Whilst Black Excellence is a reaction against archaic external stereotypes designed to limit our capabilities, excellence should not be the required standard for black people to reach in order to be *seen* within our community. Yes, let's celebrate the achievements of those in our community who go on to achieve the very best, and assume roles in changing societal narratives on blackness. However, let us also celebrate the psychological strength of the black individual who simply wakes up every day in defiance of the inferiority complex whiteness attempts to ingrain into us by devaluing the worth of our place in society. I myself have in certain spaces navigated both positions, as we all will. Mainstream society often forgets us. Let's not forget each other.

References

1 Ezra Klein, 'Sam Harris, Charles Murray, and the allure of race science', *Vox*, (27 March 2018) <https://www.vox.com/policy-and-politics/2018/3/27/15695060/sam-harris-charles-murray-race-iq-forbidden-knowledge-podcast-bell-curve>
2 *The Lost Libraries of Timbuktu*, BBC, (8 October 2018)
3 A. Moore, '11 Ancient African Writing Systems That Demolish the Myth That Black People Were Illiterate', *Atlanta Black Star*, (8 August 2014) <https://atlantablackstar.com/2014/08/08/11-ancient-african-writing-systems-demolish-myth-black-people-illiterate/4/>
4 Bill Desowitz, '"Black Panther": How Wakanda Got a Written Language as Part of its Afrofuturism', *IndieWire*, (22 February 2018)

   <https://www.indiewire.com/2018/02/black-panther-wakanda-written-language-ryan-coogler-afrofuturism-1201931252/>

5 'Ramarni Wilfred tops Bill Gates and Einstein with his IQ', BBC News, (9 January 2019) <https://www.bbc.co.uk/news/av/uk-england-london-46788534/ramarni-wilfred-tops-bill-gates-and-einstein-with-his-iq>

6 'Civilizing Mission', *Wikipedia*, ≤https://en.wikipedia.org/wiki/Civilizing_mission≥

7 ed. Claire Alexander and Jason Arday, 'Aiming Higher: Race, Inequality and Diversity in the Academy', Runnymede, (February 2015) <https://www.runnymedetrust.org/uploads/Aiming%20Higher.pdf>

8 'Oxford was more likely to offer a place to the best black candidates last year – but its race problem is more complicated than that', Channel 4, (24 May 2018) <https://www.channel4.com/news/factcheck/factcheck-oxford-is-actually-more-likely-to-offer-a-place-to-the-best-black-candidates>

9 'Anti-knife branding in chicken shops 'racist or stupid', says MP', *Guardian*, (14 August 2019) <https://www.theguardian.com/uk-news/2019/aug/14/anti-knife-branding-in-chicken-shops-called-stupid-by-mps>

10 Haroon Siddique, 'Minority ethnic Britons face "shocking" job discrimination', *Guardian*, (17 January 2019), <https://www.theguardian.com/world/2019/jan/17/minority-ethnic-britons-face-shocking-job-discrimination>

11 In its January 2018 report 'Delivering through Diversity' McKinsey & Company found that companies in the top quartile for ethnic and cultural diversity on their executive teams were 33 per cent more likely to experience above-average profitability than companies in the bottom quartile. 'Delivering through Diversity', McKinsey, (January 2018) <https://www.mckinsey.com/business-functions/organization/our-insights/delivering-through-diversity>

12 The July 2019 Office of National Statistics (ONS) report 'Ethnicity pay gaps in Great Britain: 2018' found that UK-born employees in the Black African, Caribbean or Black British ethnic group are estimated to earn 7.7 per cent less than their UK-born white British counterparts. 'Ethnicity Pay Gaps in Great Britain', Office for National Statistics, (9 July 2018) <https://www.ons.gov.uk/employmentandlabourmarket/peopleinwork/earningsandworkinghours/articles/ethnicitypaygapsingreatbritain/2018>

13 https://www.etymonline.com/word/mediocre

14 A 2016 study by Vox showed that 'Gang member' and 'thug' roles in film are disproportionately played by black actors. Zachary Crockett, '"Gang member" and "thug" roles in film are disproportionately played

by black actors', *Vox*, (13 September 2016) <https://www.vox.com/
2016/9/13/12889478/black-actors-typecasting>

15 Priscilla Frank, 'Black Women Artists Tackle The Dangerous
Stereotypes That Have Never Defined Them', *Huffington Post*,
(8 December 2016) <https://www.huffingtonpost.co.uk/entry/black-
woman-artists-stereotypes_us_58471907e4b016eb81d8868b?ri18n
=true&guccounter=1&guce_referrer=aHR0cHM6Ly9jb25ZW50Lnlh
aG9vLmNvbS8&guce_referrer_sig=AQAAANVssV_0gzaORBJa-p3X_
oEup-pReW_b6Y9_9Y6vIJNQilkvmuPcRPCdf2qvVJSEzgah6fHXmEjef
NvU0Q5Cl-jUwJTI_Y_ICmsKKcsJrJbGZp3sSX_XkWeRZWZBl9lw8pFLR
5hY7E0fT8cZU9 qp0ld2t1gGPspXwYB8y9Yz5JRA>

16 'Race and Attraction', *OkCupid* [blog], (10 September 2014) <https://
theblog.okcupid.com/race-and-attraction-2009-2014-107dcbb4f060>

17 https://www.youtube.com/watch?v=HCo3dDlrjUI&t=280s

18 In February 2019, the Labour MP criticised Stacey Dooley's
perpetuation of 'white saviour' stereotypes after her trip to Uganda for
Comic Relief in which she posted her 'obsession' with a young Ugandan
boy on her social media. Nadeem Badshaw, '"White saviour" row:
David Lammy denies snubbing Comic Relief', *Guardian*, (28 February
2019) <https://www.theguardian.com/tv-and-radio/2019/feb/28/
david-lammy-stacey-dooley-comic-relief-white-saviour-row-uganda-
red-nose-day-film>

EUNICE OLUMIDE

Often referred to as Scotland's first black supermodel, Eunice started her career in fashion, at 15, working for designers like Mulberry, Alexander Wang, Christopher Kane and Henry Holland. When she's not modelling, she's campaigning and using her voice on matters of sustainability, mental health, class and race. She is also an author: her book *How To Get Into Fashion* provides a guide to the industry, covers diversity in fashion and the A to Z of just what it takes to make it in the fashion world. You can also catch her regularly on your TV, either acting or as a broadcaster – all while splitting her time between Scotland and London. Where she finds the time to slay in her lane, we don't know!

In her essay, Eunice probes the gaps in the historical narrative and interrogates traditional representations of black women in film, television and music. She writes persuasively on the necessity for more authentic portrayals than the limited and interchangeable roles that have been made available to – or foisted upon – us up until now.

Programmed:
Transferred Representations
and Interchangeable States

The dispiritingly paltry state of black British history, with its gaping lacunae and uncomfortable relationship with the mainstream historical establishment is increasingly subject to serious challenge and research. But alongside this long overdue interrogation, we need to understand the consequences of this failure of the narrative of black culture and history, and British perceptions of it.[1] We also need to be aware of how the absence, in film and television, of a black British identity and narrative, led to a media vacuum that was then filled in the last decades of the twentieth century, by American TV shows and Hollywood movies. The result, for the media generations who came before us, was an image of the non-white, the not-us, the 'negro' that was a tragicomic travesty.

The British experience is further muddied by the nation's ambivalent role as both slaver and abolitionist, and the postwar embarrassment about empire, de-colonisation, and all its attendant paradoxes. Add to this mass immigration and a seismic demographic shift and it's not surprising that so many people have simply given up on black British history entirely, with its American style accusatory polemic, which – while cathartic for the writer – does not advance the clarity or accuracy of the discussion. Which is a pity, because we have an opportunity here to escape from the bitter emotional circularity and reclaim our own specific narrative, with all of its stories, its horrors and triumphs, and frame it anew as part of the mainstream of this island's history and its peoples, and not something separate or 'apart'. It's within this context that I want to look at transferred representations of black women from the US to the UK, not just for their own sake, but for the sake of 'invisible' women in all cultures, both past, present, and future.

Those in the African diaspora live lives refracted through the skewed black lens of African-American history. Early cinema and television have played a crucial role in creating this quagmire.[2] Back in the day of the blackface minstrel shows, African-Americans were forced to go along with these invented misconceptions, both on and off screen.[3] Consequently, many generations of people across the world believed these fictitious representations to be reality. Such as the black child depicted in the children's book, *The Little Black Sambo* (1899), or the deeply offensive name Coon being attributed to laziness. So, what's the big deal? In the decades that followed, numerous non-black historians, cultural engineers, producers and directors built their narratives on these misconceptions. Fast forward to the twenty-first century and we've been left with some stark representations of the black woman: The Mammy, The Heroine, The Ho and The Angry Black Woman. Sounds like the synopsis of a new comedy for the Edinburgh Fringe Festival?

The Mammy

If you don't know about the movie *Gone with the Wind* (1939) then get to know it. Saluted then as the ultimate guide to the picture-perfect black woman. Ignore the standard gendered domestic clichés and focus instead on Mammy. The role was played by the indelible Hattie McDaniel (who, incidentally, became the first black woman in history to receive an Oscar[4]). Astonishingly submissive, obedient, caring, able to cook Michelin-standard meals at the drop of a hat, as well as maintain an entire household of Caucasians, Mammy was the archetypal in-house slave. Of course, her own needs and kinfolk came last, if indeed she attended to them at all.

The Mammy is typically represented as overweight, dark-skinned, and comedically unattractive: that is, of course, according to Western beauty ideals. Most importantly, she does not want to be free; she is content in her life of bondage. Now, while this might be true historically in a few cases, contemporary accounts, memoirs and just plain common sense tell us that the day-to-day reality for most female slaves was very different.

To give you an idea of how revered this fictitious character was, in 1923, Congressman Charles Stedman introduced a bill on behalf of the Jefferson Davis Chapter of the UDC to erect a monument to Hattie's services. It was then authorised by the US Senate. The Mammy from *Gone with the Wind* quite literally became a national hero. Bear in mind that these were the same political structures that were actively complicit in lynching and segregation . . . so, I'm pretty sure that this effigy was not particularly effective in the pursuit of black power and independence.[5] Coincidentally, the actual place on which they proposed to build the monument is just a stone's throw away from where the current Martin Luther King statue stands today. In the end, Hattie's statue was never built, after pushback from the black community.

The Ho

During the transatlantic slave trade, black women did not own their own bodies. They were the property of their masters, and whoever those masters decided to lend them out to at any given time. Similarly, in the early nineteenth century, Sarah Baartman, the 'Hottentot Venus' was exhibited across Europe, as both an object of freakish curiosity and of sexual desire. Traditionally women have been consistently defined as an erotic object both in film and television.[6] And depictions of black women in film and television over the last centuries have consistently repeated this power dynamic in various iterations, which goes some way to explicating why in so much contemporary media, women of colour are swathed in carnal yearning, and exploited in the same fashion.

In the eighties, entertainment networks BET and MTV unashamedly pioneered the modern Ho. And today, the 'urban' music video has become the *creme de la creme* of day-time soft porn. Yes, for the last thirty years or so, hip hop has produced a veritable buffet of pimps and ass for you to get your snack on. Record labels were ruthless in their thirst to depict a salacious gangster lifestyle,[7] until it just became part and parcel of the rap industry, and as it evolved, the few black labels that existed understood that if they wanted to make *that paper* they needed *to get with the programme*. Thus dawned the age of the independent music producer, and of moguls including Dr Dre and Suge Knight constructing their empires specifically on the gangster lifestyle, incarceration, drugs, death and destitution.[8] Numero uno P.I.M.P., Snoop Dog's album *Doggy Style* (1993) was the blueprint of how to shake, sell and get ass.

If you thought things couldn't get any sexier, then fast forward to the 2000s where we are introduced to the meticulous and deeply complex artistry of T-Pain's 'Work' (2013), Trey Songz's 'Animal' (2017) and Lil Sicc's 'Face Down' (2017) (please finish the lyric!). The music video to the latter kicks off with a CPU of a woman's derriere as she struts seductively through a dingy hotel corridor into a room full of 'da man dem'. The viewer is smacked in the face with explicit scenes of sexual imagery, as another five topless dancers join the party. News flash! Are we still watching a music video? Shouldn't we be focusing on talent first, looks second?

American music videos and popular culture have sought to

erase the accomplished talent of conscious female rappers such as Roxanne (1984), in favour of hyper-sexualised virtual reality busty babes inspired by Lil Kim. Back in the nineties, West Coast hip-hop royalty dominated this scene (make way for Foxy Brown and Lil Kim). Since then, this type of representation has monopolised our airwaves and YouTube streams, from Nicky Minaj to Cardi B, Megan Thee Stallion to Dolja Cat. But in case you're worried that our toddlers and teenyboppers are missing out, don't worry, we have Ariana Grande to tickle their fancy. Most people would agree that Lauryn Hill (1990s) was the only conscious female rapper to have achieved actual worldwide commercial success. Unfortunately, her constant search for equality resulted in her being deemed wilfully belligerent, hostile, and away with the fairies (Scottish for not in her right mind), traits that will shut down a woman's career quicker than Stormzy shut down Wireless. Colourism and African-American representations of the ideal woman have continued to impregnate popular culture in the UK, highlighted in music videos such as 'Pounds OPP' (2019). In most cases black women are completely missing altogether – see Giggs' 'Sexy' (2017).

The Heroine

Think about every Marvel movie you've ever seen. Multiply that by the power of Thor and add a few shots of Athena, then you might just get close to the invincible force that is the black woman – according to the telly. She is limitless in her emotional and visceral strength and is more than delighted to help others ahead of herself. Nowhere is this clearer than in prevalent television series *Empire* (2015–). Taraji P. Henson plays a hardcore black mother, who of course has done a few decades in the 'tin pale' (Scottish for jail) on behalf of her husband, no questions asked. She maintains a formidable narcotics and musical empire, while simultaneously enduring her husband's relentless infidelity. Mother to two delinquent sons, she manages to support both *and* look good while doing it. How is this possible? The mind boggles. We also see this interchangeable character – in this case played by Netflix natural Naturi Naughton – rear her magnificent head in hit TV series *Power* (2014–).

Even when there are characters who seem to represent the black woman in a respectable manner, her invented hereditary disposition to violence, flawless ability for perfection and emasculating behaviour place her in an isolated, gilded prison. In *Scandal* (2012–) Kerry Washington plays a former White House Communications Director, but as if that is not enough for one lifetime, this superwoman and supertalent extraordinaire starts her own management firm at the drop of a hat. *How to Get Away with Murder* (2014–) sees Viola Davis deliver a dazzling performance as criminal defence lawyer Annalise Keating. Of course, she consistently saves the day, in true style, as only a black woman could. Tears? Certainly not on her watch. What these characters all have in common is their tremendous omnipotent strength and ability to go through more anguish, more strife and more punishment than anyone else, even through the shade.

The Angry Black Woman

From the nineteenth century we see the emergence of the ABW, coined in movies such as *Deliver Us from Eva* (2003). Gabrielle Union's character essentially gives up her life to look after her younger sisters, but is ultimately still depicted as hostile, uncompromising and intimidating. In return she is loathed, mocked and shunned by her family and friends.

Pumped-up adrenalin-fuelled TV series, like *The Real Housewives of Atlanta* (2006–) and *Basketball Wives* (2010–) bombard us with daily doses of black women engaged in full-on fist fights, actual bodily harm, with a wee pinch of gold digging on the side, just for that extra spicy flavour.

Diary of a Mad Black Woman (1995) was instrumental in terms of illustrating the impact of wider social issues within the black community, including the epidemic rise of black men actively dating outside of their race.[9] In the film Kimberly Elise plays the jilted wife of her high-flying husband. Out of the blue, he returns to their marital home one day and 'dashes her on road'. Translation: literally rips her out of the house and throws her face down in the gutter. Broken, bruised and devastated she miraculously rebuilds her entire life from scratch, of course completely solo, in true stereotypical black woman style. Her husband sustains a serious spinal injury, his life is hanging in the balance, and his new younger, fairer girlfriend decides she's had enough; robs all his cash and buggers off, leaving his wife behind to nurse him back to health. By anyones standards she should be hailed as a super wife, for her remarkable aptitude for grief, pain and humiliation, but as the title of the film reveals she is somehow still depicted as bitter, aggressive and just plain scary, which does seem to be just a wee bit harsh.

Cross over the pond to the United Kingdom, in 1994 and we see the emergence of one of the Western world's greatest selling girl bands, the Spice Girls, with its token black girl, conveniently dubbed 'Scary Spice'. Coincidence? Perhaps. But with so few representations of black women available, this interpretation undoubtedly supported those tropes that are commonly disseminated in Western media.

But is this all just pure entertainment? A slice of pop culture, punch-ups and nights on the piss? The problem is that these characters have overshadowed alternative representations, such as *Ama* (1991), or *Burning an Illusion* (1981), in which Cassie McFarlane plays an adroit young woman making her way in the Thatcherised hailstorm of racism and discrimination. She is a figure of strength and dignity who encompasses all the organic insecurities and nuances of real life that black women faced at that time.[10]

The Interchangeable Matters

Over the last century, television, movies and music have provided an extraordinary vehicle for the export of blackness. This catalyst has been so successful that many, regardless of their race, still believe unquestioningly in these fictional images.[11] These false portrayals have gone unchallenged, since they often do not affect the lives of the prevailing classes.[12] As ever, it is those groups with the least amount of economic power who are more likely to be alienated and misrepresented.

So how can we move forward? Firstly, we need to identify and understand the social, political and economic ramifications of these ideologies and to analyse the exploitation of the black woman in the media, for profit and entertainment – from Sarah Baartman to Hattie McDaniel's Mammy, to the present day. Then we need to promote and create compelling competing representations that are not only authentic but vary from region to region.

Secondly, we must urgently collate and archive the real-life historical contribution of women of colour, which has been largely brushed under the carpet by restrictive social and racial conventions. Outside of the highly romanticised colonial 'safari opera' of *Sanders of the River* (1935), the stories of real black women have too rarely been studied or portrayed. Stories including the life and work of Sarah Forbes Bonnetta (1843–1880), the beloved adopted daughter of Queen Victoria (1837–1901); stories of Queen Charlotte, who may have been the first black queen of England; or of Dido Elizabeth Belle, are only now being considered and told.

Thirdly, we need to continue to interrogate contemporary representations of black women and demand more authentic portrayals than the limited roles of The Mammy, The Ho, The Heroine and The Angry Black Woman. It is encouraging that there are signs that cultural producers are finally beginning to take the problem of misrepresentation seriously. Netflix, for example,[13] has committed to supporting more legitimate portraits of black life, such as the awkward, deeply religious Tracey Gordon played by Michaela Coel in *Chewing Gum* (2015–2017). But there is still a long way to go.

To be fair though, there are many pros to hyper-marginalisation, especially if you happen to be an Afro-Scot, or from a country that is not historically associated with 'blackness'. Once the world realises that unicorns do exist, this is your cue to revel in the art of getting to be whatever you want. The unwritten etiquette of society, whether high or low simply does not apply to you, since people don't have a clue how you will act or think. It's up to you to set the bar.

But for all of us, the most important way to affect change is understanding that ignorance is not bliss, it's straight up taking the piss. You can choose to conform to the norm, or you could choose to constantly reposition yourself as an educator or supporter by helping others understand the history of the African diaspora in the West, or you could simply keep being you which is just as magnificent.

References

1 Malachi McIntosh, Hannah Elias, *'Teaching BAME History as British History: What does it have to do with Brexit'*, <https://blog.history.ac.uk/2019/01/teaching-bame-history-as-british-history-what-does-it-have-to-do-with-brexit/ Institute for Historical Research 23 January 2018>

2 Anthony Giddens, Philip W. Sutton. *Essential Concepts in Sociology* 2nd Edition Polity Press 2017, p148

3 *Celebrating the Faithful Coloured Mammies of The South.* https://rediscovering-black-history.blogs.archives.gov/2013/04/04/celebrating-the-faithful-mammies-of-the-south/Tribute/News Ligon. Posted in Post-Reconstruction, Tribute/News 4 April, 2013

4 Dr David Pilgrim, Professor of Sociology, *The Mammy Caricature* https://www.ferris.edu/jimcrow/mammies/ Ferris State University October 2000 Edited 2012

5 Ibid.

6 Anthony Giddens, Philip W. Sutton, *Essential Concepts in Sociology* 2nd Edition Polity Press 2017, p148

7 Erin Blakemore. *How Race Records Turned Black Music into Big Business*, https://www.history.com/news/race-records-bessie-smith-big-bill-broonzy-music-business 22 February 2019.

8 Greg, Tate, *Gangsta Rap*, https://www.britannica.com/art/gangsta-rap Encyclopaedia Britannica 2013

9 Tera R. Hurt, Stacey E. McElroy, Kameron J. Sheats, Antoinette M. Landor, and Chalandra M. Bryant, *Married Black Men's Opinions as to Why Black Women Are Disproportionately Single: A Qualitative Study*, https://www.ncbi.nlm.nih.gov/pmc/articles/PMC4465800/ Published online Department of Human Development and Family Studies, Iowa State University, 24 August 2013.

10 Ashley Clark, *10 great black British Films*, https://www.bfi.org.uk/news-opinion/news-bfi/lists/10-great-black-british-films BFI 16 August 2018.

11 Anthony Giddens, Philip W. Sutton, *Essential Concepts in Sociology* 2nd Edition Polity Press 2017

12 Anthony Giddens, Philip W. Sutton, *Essential Concepts in Sociology* 2nd Edition Polity Press 2017, p. 147

13 Danielle Bitni, *Is Netflix The New Mecca For Black Content?* https://www.essence.com/entertainment/netflix-new-mecca-black-content/ 26 June 2018

FIONA RUTHERFORD

Fiona is a journalist we have long admired. Liz became aware of her through her coverage of the Grenfell fire, where Fiona's compassion in interviews with the Grenfell Tower survivors was moving. Though her path into journalism was accidental, Fiona has become an important voice in the industry and she's currently news editor at Bloomberg's QuickTake, and previously worked as a reporter at *BuzzFeed News*. With her background in neuroscience and psychology she also writes science pieces for other publications too. It was an honour when we found out we were finalists in the same category as Fiona at 2019's Black British Business Awards. Here she writes persuasively about the importance of financial literacy amongst black women as a way of empowering ourselves, something she believes is vital in helping us to navigate an increasingly uncertain future.

Why It's Time to Get Your Finance in Formation

I've always known that nothing would ever be handed to me on a silver plate. It's a message that has probably been drilled into every black woman – you're going to have to work even harder than everyone else because you have two strikes against you – your gender and your race. Though one thing for sure is that hard work alone is not paying off – the world still has a long way to go before we reach a point where black women are treated fairly. It's time for black women to rethink our strategy around working hard, especially what we do with the product of our hard work – the thing we don't talk about enough: money.

Black women have always faced several barriers in the workplace, and the struggle has been widely documented. The most recent findings from the Office for National Statistics show that despite holding similar qualifications black British employees are paid 7.7 per cent less than their white counterparts – one of the highest gaps among all ethnic groups. Across the Atlantic the story is the same: analysis of wage data by the American Association of University Women shows that on average black women in the US have to work at least eight months more to earn what a white man does in one year. There are a range of theories for why this is the case – racism, the historical marginalisation of black communities, unconscious bias – yet despite having the additional full-time job of navigating these barriers, black women are succeeding and excelling in a range of fields.

With that in mind, as I write this essay, I'm thinking about the various hard-working black women in my life. I'm thinking about my younger sister, who, once she graduates next year, will be entering the world of work in an industry that is notoriously dominated by men. I'm thinking about my 97-year-old grandma who came to the UK from Jamaica in the late 50s – when shop windows had signs on the doors, which read 'No Irish, No Blacks, No Dogs'. While juggling being a single mother of four, my grandma worked at a dry cleaner, amongst several other jobs, on minimum wage, ironing the shirts of the rich and famous she always reminds me. She once took on a night job to earn extra cash to help send my 13-year-old mum to typewriting school. My grandma today – relatively active, independent and still hard-working – would probably still be employed if my mum hadn't forced her to retire at the age of 80. And then there's my mum who went to university as a mature student after having my sister and me. She continues to study, loves learning new things and has not let her experience of workplace racism and bullying stop her from pursuing her passion.

Growing up I was taught to work hard – and I did – but I was never taught money skills. Black women may be smart, but when our paycheques come in, how clever are we being with what we earn? How can we be financially empowered to create a life for ourselves that makes us secure and in control? At my first paid job, age 16, I earned about £4 an hour as a cashier at McDonald's. I remember the first few days of the job being so intense that at night I would dream about the tills. I've had several jobs since then, and earning my own money felt great – I didn't need to rely on anyone else, I could buy what I wanted when I wanted. But by the time I was in my early 20s I was in thousands of pounds worth of debt. I was deep into my overdraft limit and had completely maxed-out credit cards that I was nowhere close to paying off. I wasn't even living paycheque to paycheque, I lived payday loan to payday loan – each month trying to figure out which payday loan company would accept me this time around. If that didn't work, I applied for credit cards, or increased my overdraft limit. If that was declined I would reluctantly sell my most valuable items – on eBay, in a pawn shop, or a second-hand goods store – for a fraction of what I bought them for. And if that didn't give me enough cash to last the rest of the month, I would ask to borrow money from family – I hated doing that, and it was always, always the last option. It was a chaotic way to live. One thing for sure is that nothing about the way I was living was sustainable. Unless something dramatic changed in my life, it would be a disaster waiting to happen.

Debt often creeps up on people, and my situation was no different. I was a working undergraduate with two part-time jobs, each of which paid me no more than £9 an hour – I earned a salary that was nowhere near to covering what I owed the banks. I was always living on the edge of my limit, and since I had zero savings, any unexpected expenses were a huge strain. Being in debt didn't happen overnight for me, it was gradual. Despite how it sounds, it didn't feel particularly uncomfortable, or even stressful for that matter – I had become used to my financially chaotic lifestyle. Putting aside all the pains and struggles that come with being a young person, a student and living in London – one of the world's most expensive cities – I had a relatively decent life. I had fun, I went out with friends, from the outside there was probably no indication that I was in thousands of pounds worth of debt. My debt was dispersed around different credit cards and overdrafts, which meant it was hard for me to see the scale of the problem. Looking back, the funniest thing is that I didn't even realise it myself. I wasn't in denial, it was rather a complete lack of awareness of the state of my financial situation.

Money problems aren't something people openly disclose – it can feel uncomfortable, awkward and shameful. A couple of years ago, entrepreneur Yemi Awopetu gave a short talk about financial management at Pursue Your Passion, a career development and mentorship event in London. I was in the audience, and when he asked us whether we had any savings I kept my hand down. I had none. I felt incredibly embarrassed. During the talk, he opened his wallet and showed the audience an impressive collection of loyalty cards and discount coupons. His message: you can always save something, no matter how small. But the one part of his speech that really stuck with me was the idea of being deliberate with your money: 'You have to tell your money where to go, rather than wonder where it went.'

I finally realised that I had an unhealthy relationship with money. Hearing someone talking about their personal finance and spending habits so openly, was a turning point for me. As Awopetu spoke to the crowd I found myself, for the first time, calculating the sum of my debt – each loan, overdraft, credit card. It was a suffocating feeling when I realised just how deep into debt I was. I panicked and I thought to myself, 'How did it even get this bad? How on earth can I get myself out of this situation?' Despite being rattled, I also felt inspired and energised. 'If you're not earning enough, then consider getting a better-paid job,' he said. Yes, it's easier said than done, but it got me thinking about the possibility of earning more, as opposed to only working with what I already had. It made me think about finding solutions to my problems, like using apps and prepaid budgeting cards that can help you keep an eye on what you're spending and automatically take savings from your account based on clever algorithms.

After the event I knew I had to confront my finances – I acknowledged that it would be messy, challenging, depressing – but I was ready to start the process. It was hard and I failed several times – dipping into my savings, ordering takeout instead of cooking, saying yes to that holiday with friends because I didn't want to miss out on all of the fun. It took a lot of discipline to change my spending habits – I would use the bus instead of the train, even if it meant leaving the house an hour earlier. I became a pro at finding deals and shopped in sale racks. I started saying no to social events that would push me out of my budget. I negotiated a cheaper phone contract and didn't upgrade unnecessarily. Thanks to YouTube I even learned how to do my own box braids – impressing all of my friends and essentially saving hundreds of pounds a year. I had multiple side hustles – tutoring, an Etsy shop, proofreading. Within two and a half years I pulled myself out of debt and aggressively built up some savings – it felt amazing and is one of my proudest achievements to date.

I am nowhere close to where I want to be financially, but one thing I can say is that I am now fully in control over my finances in a way I wasn't before. I know what I need to be earning in order to live the life I want for myself. I'm aware of my outgoings and incomings. I can use debt and credit to my advantage. I have savings and I am continuing to learn about financial terms and strategies. It also took a degree of what felt like selfishness – society teaches and expects women to be altruistic, selfless and self-sacrificing – so when I quit several of my voluntary, unpaid commitments it felt immensely uncomfortable. I knew I could go back to volunteering, but right now it was time to put myself first.

Back in 2016 a Billfold piece 'A Story of a Fuck Off Fund' went viral. The post, written by Paulette Perhach, shared a powerful message about what she describes as 'financial self-defense'. The story is about how the lack of a fuck off fund – a pot of emergency money – meant she stayed in an abusive relationship with her boyfriend and put up with inappropriate behaviour from her boss at work. Having a fuck off fund changed everything. She wrote:

> When your boyfriend calls you stupid, you say if he ever
> says that again, you're out of there, and it's not hard to
> imagine how you'll accomplish your getaway . . . When
> your boss attempts to grope you, you say, 'Fuck off, you
> creep!' You wave two middle fingers in the air, and march
> over to HR. Whether the system protects you or fails you,
> you will be able to take care of yourself.

The piece was a reminder to women all over the world that a bad financial situation can make you feel trapped, alone, and might lead you to make decisions that are not in your best interest. It was a wakeup call that women need to be equipped with tools to protect themselves. The examples within the story were relatable to me. Unhealthy financial situations meant that I put up with abusive behaviour because I felt like I had no choice and wouldn't be able to do any better. Financial independence gives women options and opens doors to a range of opportunities. It allows women to be picky about where they work, how much they earn and lets them take risks. Of course, healthy finances won't be a solution to all of the problems that black women will face, but being and feeling financially secure, balanced and in control will give us the opportunities needed to pursue the things we care about. Money should be a means to achieve our life goals. As Awopetu said, we should be telling our money where to go, not the other way round.

There are several black women who are spreading awareness about financial empowerment, like blogger Bola Sol whose Refined Currency platform educates women about money matters, from managing debt to improving credit scores. Melanie Eusebe, co-founder of the Black British Business Awards, launched Money Moves – a membership programme, which aims to help black communities manage and navigate wealth. Just recently Black Ballad, a platform for black women, collaborated with the *Financial Times* on an event about helping women make the most of their money. It's exciting to see such a growing movement of women acknowledging the importance of being in control of their finances – and helping other women along the way.

Looking ahead at the political and economic landscape of this country, financial empowerment, independence and health are more important than ever. The future of the UK is uncertain and scary. Just take Brexit, for example. The UK's future relationship with the EU is continuously affecting the economy, and in turn, is likely to have a disproportionate impact on women from minority ethnic backgrounds. Reports show that ethnic minorities in Britain are worse off when it comes to getting jobs, in terms of housing and are hardest hit by austerity measures. With this in mind, black women should be equipping themselves with as many tools as necessary to ensure that whatever happens, we are able to create the best possible life for ourselves. We should know our worth, and feel comfortable setting a price for our labour that allows us to live in the way we want. Financial health is not drilled into us from an early age, but now more than ever is time to make it part of our self-care regimes. Financial self-care is about having a nourishing relationship with money – using it as a device to make you happy, feel in control and obtain balance in your life. We should set aside regular time for focusing on our finances, in the same way that we think about our emotional and physical health and wellbeing.

When I finally decided to practise financial self-care, I noticed the difference in myself. It felt like a detox – my financial acne was cleared up, and my new, clearer skin was glowing, giving me a newfound confidence. Over time I saw myself become more deliberate about my spending, closing credit cards, reducing my overdraft to an amount that I could afford to pay off each month, switching to savings accounts with better interest rates. I was never any good at saving money before, I had no self-control and would regularly dip into any additional money I had. But practising financial self-care forces me to be more forward-thinking – I ask myself questions about my future, the kind of house I want to buy, what success looks like to me, and how I'd like to live during retirement.

With radical changes to my spending habits, I went from a person living with thousands of pounds worth of debt and no control over my money, to being someone who enjoyed watching their money grow – and helping other women to feel financially empowered.

When my grandad kicked my grandma and their young kids out in the street during the middle of the night, with nowhere to go, perhaps a fuck off fund would've turned the tables. I wish she'd had a fuck off fund so that she didn't have to put up with decades of racism at work just to put food on the table and pay the rent. I wish that I could go back in time and encourage my grandma to think about a retirement plan, so that as well as being around her friends and family, she could've retired much earlier than 80. I wish she was able to spend more time in her home country before she became too weak to travel. I hope my hard-working sister thinks about having savings, smart investments and using her money to live her best life – whatever that looks like to her. I hope that when it comes to negotiating a salary she knows when to walk away if the offer isn't what she wants. I hope she realises that financial empowerment is about more than just money; it's about knowing when to leave unhealthy jobs and unhealthy relationships. I hope that my mum, after years of working and studying, can use her money to live the life she deserves. I definitely get the hard-working gene from my mum – like me, she has worked continuously since she was a teenager. Unlike myself, my mum always saved money, no matter how small. Although having savings is only a good thing, I hope that black women, like my mum, feel empowered to go further with their money by investing and taking risks to generate wealth.

We all know that as black women we have to work even harder than everyone else because we're living with two strikes against us – being black and being a woman. But it's time to rethink our strategy to enable us to live our life to its fullest potential – for the generations of black women who came before us, for those black women who will come after us, but most importantly for ourselves.

JENDELLA BENSON

We've always admired Jendella and her work, especially around motherhood, parenting and family life, and it was such a pleasure to get to know her at the publication brunch for our *Slay In Your Lane Journal*. Jendella is a British Nigerian writer, photographer, filmmaker and the author of *Young Motherhood*. Her visual work has featured in the *Guardian*, the *Metro*, and the *Voice Newspaper* and has been exhibited across the UK and internationally. Here, she writes about the power that comes from owning our own narratives through recording and documenting black lives from the inside out: through literature, film, journalism, art, criticism, academia – everything.

Respect On Our Name:
From Othered To Iconic
and Beyond

I often think about the details of my childhood that my children will just never understand. One of these things is the trials of a dial-up modem. They will never know the way the hours would stretch after school as I waited for my designated sixty minutes of off-peak Internet use. As soon as 7 p.m. hit I was ready to click 'connect' and listen to the screeching call-and-response of our modem connecting to the 'information superhighway'. That was the Internet that I grew up on.

This was back in the day when we were all anonymous by default. Social media didn't exist as it does now, but we communicated with strangers in forums and chat rooms, where you would choose a username like 'koolgurl88' or 'backstreet4eva976' and your avatar was often just an image chosen from a preset selection. No one's picture was online unless you were famous, or a porn star.

Back then the Internet wasn't an extension of the real world. It was its own realm entirely. I didn't expect to find school friends or family members lurking in the hundreds of pages of threaded forum posts, and even if they had been there, I wouldn't have known which pixelated avatar they were behind. Back then, the point of the Internet was to talk to people you wouldn't be able to talk to in real life.

For me, this meant a chance to shapeshift. Up until that point, I had spent much of my life as the one black face amongst a sea of white. At my primary school, in a mostly white lower-middle-class/working-class area, I was the black girl with the plaits that boys would call turds. In secondary school, there was one black girl carefully deposited in each class so although I got on well with the other black girls in my year, my closest friends were either Asian or white.

Logging onto the World Wide Web, with all of our anonymous identities, I had no reason to believe things were any different elsewhere. The world out there was white, I believed, and I knew the unspoken limitations and assumptions that came by inhabiting the body of a lanky, unattractive, awkward black girl in real life, so why not ditch all of that baggage when I had the chance? I could just pretend that I was someone else.

To be fair, this wasn't a new idea. I had been plagued by my 'otherness' from a young age. At one point I remember using my pink Lycra ballet skirt as a 'wig' and playing imaginary games where I was a little white girl in a red T-shirt and blue jeans who would go on 'adventures'. My imagination could turn my front room into a world of mountains and forests as easily as it could make my ballet skirt into silky blonde hair. So as embarrassing as it is to recall all this now as a woman in my early 30s, a pre-teen version of me going onto forums pretending to be a brunette called Nikki was nothing new.

As time went on and I graduated from forums to mastering HTML and building my own websites, I matured and started using the Internet as myself. 'Jeni' appeared in usernames and my profiles were populated with what I thought were the most interesting things about me: my birthstone, my favourite clothing stores and whether I preferred pizza or Chinese food. I built enough trust with an Internet friend in San Francisco, and she let me become one of her 'subbies', creating a sub-domain attached to her main domain for me to use: a prime bit of Internet real estate for someone whose parents would not allow her to purchase a domain of her own.

In conversation with this San Franciscan I remember mentioning in passing the fact that I was actually black. Maybe the pause in the flow of conversation was imagined, maybe my friend had left her keyboard to grab a snack or use the toilet, but the 'Oh, cool' she eventually replied with meant something more than simply 'Oh, cool'. There was surprise encoded somewhere in those two words, I was sure of it.

By the time social media became a 'thing' and we had found ways to put pictures of ourselves easily online, I was discovering that the world was not as white as I had imagined. Mainly because I had moved to a sixth form college whose demographic allowed me to join a group of loud and lively black friends. But I was also now connecting with other black teenagers from across the UK and America on Bebo, Hi5 and eventually MySpace. Things really changed though, when I was at university and I discovered Tumblr and Black Feminism.

These two discoveries were initially separate. I studied design and photography but through my art history class and eventually my dissertation I began to learn about concepts such as 'the white male gaze'. I started taking out books from the library by bell hooks and Patricia Hill Collins and somehow stumbled upon a Google Groups email thread made up of Black Feminists in London, eventually convincing my best friend to accompany me to monthly meetings where we thought we might be judged for our relaxed hair (we weren't).

Around that time I was also falling deeper into the world of Tumblr, a maze of blogs where all manner of subcultures intersected in a colourful explosion of gifs, memes and posts entirely in lower case. I followed accounts called 'fuckyeahblackgirls' and 'fuckyeahdiverseafrica'; accounts devoted to black female rappers, micropoetry and every other niche that sparked my interest.

This was where I discovered the hashtags #teamnatural, #carefreeblackgirl and #blackgirlmagic, and the international community of young black women who congregated around them, and it was where I began to truly appreciate that 'blackness' was a language, a kind of cultural currency that cuts across nations and continents. Here is where I learned – through long, unpunctuated posts and short, witty interactions – that I wasn't the only young black woman awakening to a new form of self-awareness and political consciousness. I was one of many realising how our individual experiences were somehow interlinked. Tumblr was an anarchic utopia of new ideas, nostalgia and the unapologetic, loud-and-proud blackness that is now so commonplace that non-black people adopt it, whether consciously or unconsciously, for 'clout'.

It's hard to describe what this corner of the Internet meant to me. Going from environments where being 'The Only Black Girl' felt like a social obstacle, to being in this digital bubble where being a 'Loud Black Girl' was the default, celebrated setting, I revelled in all of it. And then this world began spilling out from Tumblr and into the world of Twitter, where being silent was not an option and the thoughts and opinions of so many of us were catapulted by retweets into the consciousness of the mainstream.

From this digital den, real-world change emerged. #BlackLivesMatter was a worldwide movement and #OscarsSoWhite shamed Hollywood into recognising its coddled biases. #MeToo – originally started by Tarana Burke but pushed further into the spotlight in the wake of Harvey Weinstein – really set the table shaking, while decolonisation movements have hit university campuses across the world, challenging everything from their reading lists to the statues enshrined on their grounds. Many, if not most, of these movements are led by black women of various ages, carried along by a spirit that doesn't allow us to consider for a second that our voices shouldn't be heard when we decide that we want to speak. We are visible and celebrated in a way that 13-year-old me with her multiple digital personas could not fathom. But this visibility has come at a price.

Amnesty International's 'Troll Patrol Report' released in December 2018 found that visible black female journalists and politicians were receiving 84 per cent more abuse than their white counterparts online. During the 2017 British election campaign, Diane Abbott – currently the longest serving black MP – received such a torrent of abuse that she had to take a step back due to ill health and has since spoken out about the toll that this abuse can take on an individual.

Seyi Akiwowo was the youngest council member ever to be elected when she joined Newham Council at 23 years old. She set out to democratise politics by documenting her work on social media, but this heightened visibility only made her a target for troll attacks that she says were 'far too slick to not be considered organised activities' in a conversation with writer Esme Allman about online abuse.[1] Her experience, and the lack of interest shown by social media platforms when she reported her harassers, led her to set up Glitch, a non-profit organisation, campaigning to end online abuse.

But it's not just public figures who are on the receiving end of digital harassment. Any vocal black woman expressing her opinion on issues of race, gender or even just posting pictures celebrating other beautiful black women can be targeted. Some women change their profile pictures to disguise their ethnicity and gender, with one Twitter user identifying only as Sydette, telling AlterNet[2] that when she switched her profile picture to an image of a white man the abuse she faced online virtually disappeared.

The consequence of hypervisibility is something that I've thought a lot about, debating whether the gains of being vocal and visible are worth the trade-offs. I wrote about this a few years ago[3] and even though I ended my essay on a defiant note, my dedication to that fearlessness has been ambivalent. Because while on the one hand things are getting so much better for black women in terms of access and opportunity, when it comes to the general tone and direction of public discourse, especially online, things are also getting much, much worse.

In the wake of the 2016 US Presidential Election and British EU Referendum, there has been a rise in reported targeted racial harassment across the West. Even in countries without such obvious political moments, there has been an increase in the prominence of far-right figures and political groups. This has changed the tone of public conversation, as closeted bigots have felt emboldened to talk and act more brazenly in line with their racist views, both online and off. When I was in my early teens, the Internet felt like a separate escape hatch from real life, but now the interconnectedness promised by the early dreams of cyberspace has turned into a real-life nightmare, where online hateful screeds inspire white men to turn up in public spaces with guns and the desire to harm.

As disheartening as this climate is, we shouldn't be surprised. This is the dance of history, with progressive leaps forward being met with vicious opposition from those wishing to keep the status quo. This can most easily be seen in American history, where after the emancipation of enslaved African Americans, Jim Crow laws enforced segregation and brutal legalised discrimination. Similarly, after the landmark *Brown* v. *Board of Education* case made the integration of schools law, governors in some southern states quietly introduced legal classifications that still marginalised black students and laid the groundwork for the inequality that exists in the American public school system to this day. After the Black Power movement of the 1970s, the 1980s brought the 'War on Drugs' that turned millions of young black men into meat to feed the Prison Industrial Complex. As it has often been characterised, progress is two steps forward, and one step back.

With this sobering reality in mind, I believe there is still plenty that we *should* be doing, but firstly, I want to take a moment to look at what we *shouldn't*. Because as the dearly departed Toni Morrison famously said, 'racism is a distraction' and in the age of never-ending notifications, distraction is easier than ever.

There is a running theory that, as they wake up to how powerful the voices of black women in particular are becoming, some brands are using 'black outrage' as a marketing gimmick. Namely, they create some insensitive or tone-deaf campaign, unleash it on the unsuspecting public and wait for Black Twitter to get enraged. This outrage then brings more awareness to the brand and the product in question, because nothing spreads as quickly as bad news. Some call this 'black outrage marketing', and whether it exists as a cynical scheme by overpaid marketing executives, or it's just the obvious outcome of a room full of hapless (usually white and middle-class) professionals trying to tap into an organic and infectious culture, is an argument for another day. But what isn't up for debate is the way that such episodes can entirely suck the air and energy out of all of us. And for the most part, no one – besides the brand and the news media sites aggregating tweets for clickbait – is getting paid.

In a similar vein, I've seen time and again black women with large followings being tagged by followers and bystanders in an attempt to get them to rage on the stranger's behalf about a particular injustice. I've often found myself in the position of being approached by editors to write on certain subjects, and feeling as though they are only asking me because they are looking for a black woman to shout eloquently about some trending topic, bringing eyeballs to websites and ticking a box for diversity along the way. A double-pat on the back for their publication, while I'm still waiting ninety days on an invoice and feeling emotionally spent from raging for hire and the negative responses that will inevitably come my way after the piece goes live.

The hypervisibility of black women has also produced a whole other set of side effects that vary from ridiculous to actually harmful. 'Digital blackface' is a term that spans a wide range of phenomena cropping up online, from non-black people using darker-skinned emojis and gifs featuring black people as proxies for their own expression, through to white people pretending to be actual black people – often black women – on social media. At the end of 2018, a number of popular Instagrammers were accused of 'blackfishing', or appropriating the look of black women to, at the very least, present as racially ambiguous, if not as a mixed-race or light-skinned black woman. More disappointingly, it was recently revealed that a popular Twitter personality, @emoblackthot, despite presenting themselves as a black woman for four years, was actually a black man.

People using 'black women's perceived social capital and voice . . . as cosplay' is a form of erasure, as expertly explained in the *Fader*'s roundtable discussion on @emoblackthot.[4] One of the contributors, Wanna Thompson, described how infuriating it is to see other people appropriate approximations of black women's identities for their own gain, when being a real, vocal black woman on the Internet comes with so much hostility.

Then there's the fact that we have seen, time and again, how black women's cultural production has been co-opted without compensation, which leaves a particularly bitter aftertaste. This happened most famously in the case of Kayla Newman, aka Peaches Monroe, the young woman behind the viral video that launched 'on fleek' into popular culture. The phrase went on to be used in campaigns by corporations flogging everything from fast fashion to fast food without so much as a nod back to the original creator. More recently, after years of back-and-forth and fending off an army of Lizzo stans, Black British singer Mina Lioness was finally credited as a co-writer on the track 'Truth Hurts', after Lizzo included one of her viral tweets word for word in the opening lyrics.

All of these phenomena I have mentioned are things to feel strongly about, and I am a fan of the well-executed and strategic 'dragging' of deserving parties, but the scale and frequency of this recurring nonsense means that if we – even the collective 'we' – were to address every instance, it would deplete us. And our energy is much needed elsewhere.

Now that we have firmly established the significance of our place in the current cultural landscape, what's next? I believe that we should focus our energies on complete ownership of our works and cultural output, our narratives and our histories, in a way that ensures that future erasure of our labour or mis-accreditation of our efforts will be impossible, even for the most determined detractor.

One criticism of this new wave of black female voices is that we have not paid homage or acknowledged the labours of our fore-mothers, and in general, it can often feel like intergenerational exchange is not as common as it should be. But one thing I dis-covered when I attempted to look into the archives, is how much of the work of Black British women from previous generations is out of print or inaccessible due to lack of reach or a straight-up lack of record. This deficiency means we have no way of fully understanding what has been lost.

These women were working in a different time, before the developments in technology and infrastructure that have levelled playing fields and demolished barriers to entry. In her essay in the *Guardian*, Booker Prize-winner Bernardine Evaristo ruminates on the recent strides that have been made by Black British women in publishing: 'I wonder what my generation might have achieved had social media been around when we were in our twenties,' she writes. 'How would our lives have been enriched by the rapid interconnectivity of today?'[5] But while we have the benefit of these privately owned portals making everything urgent and immediate, we must be sure to add to the catalogue of history that will continue to exist should these platforms go away.

We cannot afford for our stories to be whitewashed. We cannot afford to let the work of those who came before us continue to be buried. As well as documenting our own efforts we should be carrying the torch forward. Zora Neale Hurston's novels would have remained lost to time if Alice Walker hadn't revived interest in her work in the 1970s. Thankfully we are beginning to see more and more black women authors get published, covering topics as varied as motherhood, love and romance and the lives of black women in post-war Britain.

I am also excited by the work being done in art and cultural criticism by women like Bolanie Tajudeen and Lisa Anderson, championing the work of Black British artists across the generations. There are black women, such as Natasha Gordon and Theresa Ikoko, writing in the realm of theatre and ensuring our experiences make it to the stage. Just as importantly there are black women behind the scenes at publishing houses, production companies, museums and galleries, and working as agents, mentors and managers – all vital roles that will forever change the face of British culture in general, for this generation and beyond. All of these efforts combine to create a rich tapestry, which is the DNA of our culture.

We live in exciting times, of that I am sure, and while the Internet that was once a playground transforms into a hellscape, we can be confident that the key desire of those wishing to attack us will never be realised. Even as some of us retreat from the cesspit of social media for our own wellbeing, the truth is that black women will never again be suppressed. Our words and our work, whether in books, on canvas, on film or on our own digital platforms, will be immortal; we're long past the point where being silenced is even a remote possibility.

References

1 Esme Allman, 'The Dark Side of Social Media for Black Women', Black Ballad, (14/02/2019) <https://blackballad.co.uk/people/the-dark-side-of-social-media-for-black-women>

2 Terrrell Jermaine Starr, 'The Unbelievable Harassment Black Women Face Daily on Twitter', AlterNet, (16/09/2014) <https://www.alternet.org/2014/09/unbelievable-harassment-black-women-face-daily-twitter/>

3 Jendella Benson, 'Is It Worth it?: Black Women's Voices and the Permission to Speak', HuffPost, (24/03/2016) <https://www.huffingtonpost.co.uk/jendella-benson/black-women-voices_b_9519060.html>

4 Clarissa Brooks, Wanna Thompson, Najma Sharif, 'How the EmoBlackThot debacle puts Black women in harm's way', Fader, (18/10/2019) <https://www.thefader.com/2019/10/18/emoblackthot-discussion-essay-isaiah-hickland>

5 Bernardine Evaristo, 'Bernardine Evaristo: "These are unprecedented times for black female writers"', *Guardian*, (19/10/2019) <https://www.theguardian.com/books/2019/oct/19/bernadine-evaristo-what-a-time-to-be-a-black-british-womxn-writer>

KUBA SHAND-BAPTISTE

Kuba is a journalist and a commissioning editor on the *Independent*'s Voices desk. In her essay, she writes powerfully – and mouthwateringly – about the politics of race, food and class amongst (in her case, second-generation) black women. She confronts her previous unhealthy relationship with Caribbean food and celebrates the way that it has now become as fundamental to her identity as her name.

Eating Britain's Racism

If the full, peppery, sharp smell of oxtail meat braising in thick, hot metal has ever made the fine hairs on the back of your neck stand to attention, you know the dish well. You know what each sound means: first the shallow fizz and heat of onions and garlic and scotch bonnet and thyme, then the deep sizzle of browning meat, followed by the hush of broth, where it rests for hours. You know what it is to wrap your lips around the finished product; how the meat falls away in thick, stringy clumps, how the brown stew and butterbeans and spinners cling to the rice it's served with like glue. How satisfied you feel once it's sitting on a plate in front of you, steaming.

I've not always felt this way about dishes like these – the ones that hail from my mother and paternal grandparents' respective homelands: Jamaica, my mother's home through birth; and Antigua, by way of Leicester, in the case of my father and his parents.

Despite the relative popularity of Caribbean food in the west – the zeal for watered-down (usually Jamaican) favourites: curry chicken, patties, fried dumplings, 'jerk' *anything*, even rice – from a very early age I drank in the social cues that told me this cuisine should be restricted to novelty consumption. It was to be eaten only at carnivals once or twice a year, in palatable, bastardised form, where the curry is mild and the meat is bony, when the

93

words 'cow foot', 'guinep', 'fungi', 'ducana', or, up until recently, 'oxtail' daren't be mentioned.

No one made it clear to me in explicit terms. Like other manifestations of socially influenced self-loathing, the understanding that 'our food' was bad, unhealthy, indulgent and that 'theirs' – with its distinct lack of flavour and much quicker preparation time – was good, had set in early enough for me to stop zealously sucking on bone marrow in company by the age of around eight. Early enough to take to shooting judgemental glances at my own mother behind her back, for failing to let the sense of shame stop her from doing the same.

While my love for what we consumed didn't necessarily diminish, by the time I was able to walk, talk and read, I already understood that the small joys of 'helping' my mother to scale fish on Saturday mornings (in reality, poking at the fish's eyes when she wasn't looking, inspecting its gills and making its mouth move) or learning how to wash milky, starched rice until the water was clear (mining for those pesky grains with the black speckles) were to remain private.

These small rituals, these dull, in many respects, everyday occurrences, were to be enjoyed in the company of family only, or among other West Indians, or anyone who frequented black and South Asian greengrocers chocabloc with green bananas, plantain, yam, cornmeal, spices and just about every foreign powdered drink you could find.

Soon, my insatiable appetite for the warm, hearty Jamaican porridges my mother painstakingly prepared for me – banana, cornmeal, you name it – waned. I wanted cereal or toast or those eggy soldier things *only*. And for dinner, no ackee and saltfish or callaloo or stew peas or snapper or rice and peas; I wanted (but of course, didn't always get) pasta. Tuna pasta. And something green and salty called pesto, a sauce I knew so little about after having tried it for the first time at a childhood friend's house that I thought it customary to mix it with ketchup.

My mother had a hard time adjusting to these strange new requests at first, too. Unfamiliar with preparing her child for sleepovers at the homes of middle-class folk who referred to dinner as 'supper', and sent their kids to bed at 6.30 p.m., she'd pack me lunch with food that she assumed would be familiar to them: the pesto and pasta with ketchup I liked so much. Until one of the parents kindly informed her that it wasn't necessary: they'd feed me and their own child with the food they'd prepared, it was no bother.

What I hadn't realised then, was that this wasn't a natural maturing of the palate, a sudden taste for all that is unmarinated. It was embarrassment, a result of learning through proximity to some of my white peers with their wildly disparate homelife; through television, which frequently warned of the damaging nature of Caribbean food and the lazy, diabetic 'fatties' who just couldn't get enough of it; and, in general, through absorbing the idea that anything we touched was, at its heart, inferior.

Even if, intellectually speaking, I knew it not to be true, thanks to the dogged home lessons from my parents, who were eager to introduce me to the likes of Nanny Maroon and Marcus Garvey, the atrocities of apartheid in South Africa, and the rich tapestry of food from around the world – deep down, I associated one of the biggest facets of the cultures that make me who I am, with abject ugliness. An ugliness I then translated into what I looked like – too black, too fat – as headlines and articles about the inherent unhealthiness of the, in reality, wildly varied dishes of the dozens of nations that make up the Caribbean, flooded the media and parts of the medical community.[12]

As I grew up, I felt as though everywhere I looked, the paunches and back rolls of fat people of all cultures were plastered all over our television and on the front pages of newspapers. I saw them ridiculed and berated for daring to breathe, with garish statistics and words like 'FAT' and 'HEART ATTACK' superimposed over their unsuspecting bodies. But what really stood out, possibly owing to my proximity to the criticism, was the notion that so-called 'African' and 'Caribbean' food, was unhealthy. Not only would it turn you into one of those headless, waddling bodies filmed without their consent on the news (bodies that looked like my own), it was also apparently being prepared by people who had no idea what they were doing.

Happily, and after many painful intervening years, by the time I was 18, my love for our food had long returned. I no longer picked out the red kidney beans from rice and peas; I had absorbed some of my mother's envied culinary skills, making curries and brown stew chicken that tasted, if I may say so myself, almost as good as hers. I could cook rice – almost any kind – with my eyes closed. And years of being instructed to boil and drain (and boil and drain again, and again) saltfish while she was still at work, to cut the sweet peppers, to saute ackee in spices, had helped quite a bit too. Finally, I was in love: with my culture, with my heritage and slowly, after years of thinking it impossible, with the body that drank it all in.

In that same year, and the years that followed, some interesting studies were published.

Commissioned by former prime minister Gordon Brown, and subsequently released during the Conservative Party and Liberal Democrat coalition government under David Cameron and Nick Clegg in 2010, epidemiologist Sir Michael Marmot wrote a review examining health inequalities in England.[3] Its aim: to redress the imbalance of government policy approaches when it came to public health, which tended to '[focus] resources only on some segments of society' and to take action to reduce that inequity 'across the social gradient'.

Some of the most interesting findings of that report include facts that many of us know and accept: that 'health inequalities arise from a complex interaction of many factors – housing, income, education, social isolation, disability – all of which are strongly affected by one's economic and social status'. And that people 'living in the poorest neighbourhoods will, on average die seven years earlier than people living in the richest neighbourhoods' – a gap that has widened since.

But despite *some* of the recommendations of the report being adopted into public policy, three years after its release, the coalition government pressed on with its gruelling programme of austerity and roundly ignored the social and economic benefits of improving prospects for the population. And who was hit the hardest? Poor people, whose suffering under the ruthless axing of public services was explained away as a necessary economic measure, while in turn doing nothing to improve growth whatsoever.[4]

After a decade of the UK's austerity programme, ironically branded as a means of ushering in a new age of pragmatism, as opposed to the 'age of irresponsibility' under the previous Labour government,[5] the damage has spiralled out of control. Homeless deaths have shattered records almost year on year; the housing crisis shows no sign of waning; the use of food banks has risen; access to mental health services has been slashed; and, as always seems to be the case, black and Asian women have been disproportionately more affected than any other group, as research from the Women's Budget Group and Runnymede Trust demonstrated in 2016.

In response to these statistics, Dr Eva Neitzart, then director of the Women's Budget Group, echoed the findings of the Marmot review and said:

> The government has repeatedly failed to carry out a meaningful analysis of the impact of their policies on different groups in society. This analysis both shows that it is technically possible and demonstrates its vital importance. It shows how the experience of austerity is determined by the combined interaction of one's income, one's gender and one's ethnicity.

In an interview with the *Guardian*'s Tim Smedley in 2013, Marmot said: 'Cutting services is regressive in its impact – higher income people use services less than lower income people. I think it's pretty clear that you can't cut budgets in local government by up to 28 per cent and [not] impact on people at economic or social disadvantage.'

Despite this, a year after the Marmot review had come out, another study from the *British Medical Journal*, in response to a 2006 paper on 'Hypertension and ethnic group', gained significant traction: 'Shocking levels of salt in African and Caribbean foods', a survey by University College London's Dr Derin Balogun.[6]

The study's aim was to look at the impact of things like processed and added salts in African and Caribbean cooking (arguably an industry and public health issue) in order to explain why 'Black people of African descent living in Britain are three to four times more likely to have high blood pressure than the white population', as well as other (possibly) dietary-related health complications. It was picked up everywhere. With quotes like this, from Dr Balogun: 'Some of the foods that [African and Caribbean people] love could be hurting the health of their hearts', and led to pushes for campaigners to specifically target the black British population, despite the prevalence of high salt consumption across the entire nation.

Crucially, it glossed over some incredibly important context: that 'staggering amounts of salt were found in dishes' that had actually been 'served in African and Caribbean restaurants' in eleven London boroughs, rather than in the home cooking of African and Caribbean people across the country.

Rather than examining the impact of economic status on lifestyle and health (as well as the fact that women of colour are more likely than any other group to live in low-income households), in the two or three years following the Marmot report, a sense of mysticism was once again foisted on to these communities, making it seem as though the seemingly 'strange' and 'backwards' practices of millions of people were really to blame for government-sanctioned inequality, and all the issues that come with it, including poor health.

What also followed, as it has increasingly over the years,[7] was the heightened demonisation of the obese, and by extension, due to perceived higher levels of obesity among them, black Brits. This may worsen significantly if the UK is to continue down the divisive, Brexit-preoccupied path it is relentlessly charging down, with no thought to the impact it will more than likely have on goods, medical supplies and the economy, whether or not we crash out.[8]

While the notion of improving health for everyone is important, the current approach – ineffective, cruel and unforgiving campaigns reliant on shame to somehow spark lifestyle changes among a group of people who are not all likely to be fat for the exact same reason (unshakable laziness and ignorance is implied) – is based on what many have referred to as the racist roots of the measurement system (Body Mass Index (BMI)) that determines what obesity actually is.

Adolphe Quetelet, an academic with no background in medicine, invented the BMI (then known as Quetelet's Index) around two centuries ago. As anonymous writer and *SELF Magazine* columnist, Your Fat Friend, wrote in October 2019, 'It was never intended as a measure of individual body fat, build, or health', but was later adopted by researcher Ancel Keys in a key study used to determine the 'most effective' medical measurement of body fat. As with Quetelet's studies, which centred on French and Scottish people, 'whiteness took center stage' in Keys' and his collaborators' research, which found that of three unreliable measurements of body fat, Quetelet's was only able to diagnose '[obesity] about 50 per cent of the time'.[9]

Not only that, but according to Georgine Leung's research, 'Diets of minority ethnic groups in the UK', which cites another 2011 study by epidemiologist Claire Nightingale, 'BMI underestimates body fatness in South Asian children but over-estimates levels of body fat in Black African-Caribbeans (because African-Caribbean children are generally taller and BMI and height are often correlated in childhood/adolescence).'[10][11]

Clearly, the methods we've long relied on for determining whether or not certain communities live up to narrow, European standards, are flawed. But the purpose of enforcing these ideals has nothing to do with accuracy, and everything to do with white supremacist reasoning. Just as nineteenth century colonisers deemed the appreciation of larger and different body types across a number of African and Asian nations as evidence of 'savagery', we still do, albeit less explicitly, today. In fact, as writer Livia Gershon points out, European colonisers tended to associate fatness with African people 'even when [they] were not at all overweight', sometimes going as far as to describe nomadic people as having 'obesity of the mind' due to a perceived lack of hard work on their end.[12] It's the same thinking when it comes to the way we discuss certain communities' cuisines.

What the many articles and reports about the dangers of Caribbean and African food specifically, also fail to address is the fact that African and Caribbean people do not necessarily consume any more salt than other groups in the UK.[13] And while there is an urgent need to promote healthy food for everyone, framing Britain's love affair with salt and sugar as a distinctly black and in some cases, Asian issue, again, rather than an economic issue, is misinformation at best.

Rather than highlighting the fact that the UK at large has considerably upped salt consumption over the years, with the diets of many 'second generation offspring of former migrants appearing to adopt British patterns, increasing fat and reducing vegetable, fruit and pulse consumption compared with first generation migrants', according to NICE,[14] the common practice of singling out specific ethnic groups and what were perceived to be their backwards practices had the media salivating.

So, too, did the notion that black women were somehow encouraged to be fat, because, as numerous health organisations, including the British Heart Foundation, suggests, 'Larger female body shapes are more likely to be seen as something to aspire to. There is therefore less pressure for women to lose weight.'[15] This is an attitude that contributes to the myth that body issues and eating disorders among black women are non-existent and should not be addressed. It's also a major factor in why fat people in general are less likely to seek medical help when they need it, instead opting for the myriad diet and self-help options that continue to make a fortune off their suffering.

It was no surprise then, that as a young teenager I had found myself deep in the throes of what I now realise was an eating disorder: rewarding myself for eating very little during the day, then binging at night until I needed to throw up in the early hours of the morning. I cried in disgust in front of the mirror when my – more common than I realised – stretch marks emerged on the sides of my stomach; punishment for not trying hard enough to starve myself. This disgust then inevitably pushed me to eat more, and to hide that consumption from others. I took pride in not finishing the 'black soup' (yam, sweet potato, boiled plantain, dumplings and chicken) my mother served me at dinnertime. Later on, I'd hate myself for not extending that level of control to junk food, all British brands, without a hint of Caribbean or African influence.

I now know how backwards that was. But it has taken years of self-reflection to come to this realisation, even if nowadays the nation has fallen back in love with 'Caribbean food', notably served in restaurant chains owned by people who do not hail from the region at all, but have capitalised on repackaging it as an 'elevated' cuisine – serving curry goat far saltier than I've ever had at home.

Even today, I still fear for future attitudes towards and biases against, not just the food, eating habits and bodies of people like me, but also for others whose entire identities are also currently under attack. The premise of the 'uneducated minority' is an attractive one, particularly in times of heightened division like these. They may tell me my food is better with a dash of 'fusion', or corporate backing, but I know they are wrong. It is the sizzling of offal, the clove-like stench of pimento, the love I had to learn again for the cultures I came from that makes it special – and it's perfect just the way it is.

References

1 'Heart fears over salty Afro-Caribbean meals', *Metro*, (2 February 2011) <https://metro.co.uk/2011/02/02/heart-fears-over-salty-afro-caribbean-meals-635890/>

2 Goff, L., Timbers, L., Style, H., & Knight, A., 'Dietary intake in Black British adults; an observational assessment of nutritional composition and the role of traditional foods in UK Caribbean and West African diets', *Public Health Nutrition*, *18*(12), 2191–2201, (August 2015) doi:10.1017/S1368980014002584

3 Michael Marmot, Peter Goldblatt, Jessica Allen, et al., 'Fair Society Healthy Lives' (The Marmot Review), Institute of Health Equity, (February 2010) <http://www.instituteofhealthequity.org/resources-reports/fair-society-healthy-lives-the-marmot-review>

4 Jonathan D. Ostry, Prakash Loungani, and Davide Furceri, 'Neoliberalism: Oversold?', *Finance and Development*, 53 (2), (June 2016) <https://www.imf.org/external/pubs/ft/fandd/2016/06/ostry.htm>

5 Nicholas Watt, 'David Cameron makes leaner state a permanent goal', *Guardian*, (12 November 2013) <https://www.theguardian.com/politics/2013/nov/11/david-cameron-policy-shift-leaner-efficient-state>

6 Morris J. Brown, 'Hypertension and ethnic group', *BMJ 332: 833*, (2016), <https://www.bmj.com/content/332/7545/833>

7 Flint, S. W., Hudson, J., & Lavallee, D. (2015). 'UK adults' implicit and explicit attitudes towards obesity: a cross-sectional study'. *BMC obesity*, 2, 31, https://doi.org/10.1186/s40608-015-0064-2

8 Gatineau M, Mathrani S., *Obesity and Ethnicity*, Oxford: National Obesity Observatory, 2011

9 'The Bizarre and Racist History of the BMI', *Medium*, (15 October 2015) <https://elemental.medium.com/the-bizarre-and-racist-history-of-the-bmi-7d8dc2aa33bb>

10 Leung, G. and Stanner, S. (2011), 'Diets of minority ethnic groups in the UK: influence on chronic disease risk and implications for prevention'. *Nutrition Bulletin*, 36: 161–198.doi:10.1111/j.1467–3010.2011. 01889.x

11 Nightingale, C. M., Rudnicka, A. R., Owen, C. G., Cook, D. G., & Whincup, P. H. (2011), 'Patterns of body size and adiposity among UK children of South Asian, black African-Caribbean and white European origin: Child Heart And health Study in England' (CHASE Study). *International Journal of Epidemiology*, 40(1), 33–44. https://doi.org/10. 1093/ije/dyq180

12 Livia Gershon, 'How Colonialism Shaped Body Shaming', *Jstor Daily*, (30 August 2019) <https://daily.jstor.org/how-colonialism-shaped-body-shaming/>

13 'How African Caribbean background can affect your health', British Heart Foundation, <https://www.bhf.org.uk/informationsupport/heart-matters-magazine/medical/african-caribbean-background-and-heart-health>

14 'Obesity: The Prevention, Identification, Assessment and Management of Overweight and Obesity in Adults and Children', Centre for Public Health Excellence at NICE (UK), (December 2006) <https://www.nice.org.uk/guidance/cg189/evidence/obesity-update-appendix-m-pdf-6960327447>

15 'How African Caribbean background can affect your health', British Heart Foundation, <https://www.bhf.org.uk/informationsupport/heart-matters-magazine/medical/african-caribbean-background-and-heart-health>

KUCHENGA

Kuchenga is a writer, a journalist and an avid reader of black women's literature as a matter of survival. She is a black transsexual feminist whose work seeks to cleave souls open with truth and sincerity. Her writing is vulnerable, powerful and inspiring. Here she writes movingly about black love and reflects on her relationship with black men as a transsexual woman. She sees the potential for black love as a redemptive soothing for the psychic damage inflicted by trauma.

I Love Us For Real: A call for a radical reconfiguration of black love from a black trans woman's perspective

> I thought I'd seen it all . . . I learned to let it go
> . . . Now I'm living the best case scenario.
>
> Shea Diamond

> L'utopie est le vérité de demain.
>
> Victor Hugo

I give black men extra leeway. My mother taught me to. Through her eyes, patriarchy looked like some experiment once voted on thousands of years ago. 'How about we give this a try for a giggle?' It was never meant to last.

Under her breath, at least once a week, she would mutter with resignation, 'Men are weak.' Nothing to do with physical strength of course. Sure, if something heavy needs lifting, then get the one with the brute muscular strength to huff and puff his way into being publicly celebrated. But underneath the bravado she would show me the scared little boy who did not have our endurance. No understanding of how to run a home with military precision, without evicting any spiritual warmth. Not as well versed in how to take care of people holistically without requiring thanks to be poured into their ego at regular intervals. Filtered through her intellectual disdain, the beastly boom of fatherly rage was revealed to be merely 'bravado unmasked'; the bass in his voice poorly disguising the fact that he was quite frazzled. 'It's just his nature. That's what he's like.' Man's volatile anger, when not dignified with the veneer of neutrality was just hysteria with extra punch. Testosterone? An unfortunate hormonal injection, replacing reason with ill-considered, thoughtless reaction.

We shuffled around Daddy's depression, leaving him to thick books and newspapers, waiting for his mood to lift him out from under his bridge, where he always forgot to moisturise his feet if we didn't remind him. At a glance I could see, because of her, that his approach to taking care of himself was slapdash. So how could this handsome ogre hope to take care of us? Who decided to let him rule our world?

Before my mother's intervention, I was very traditionalist. If I am being honest, in a number of ways I still am. When it comes to my romantic relationships, I am what Kimberly Foster, the founder of the online platform *For Harriet*, calls 'a feminist in the streets and a pick me in the sheets'. I began to gender the world under instruction from the media. In Muswell Hill, at our family friends' house, I expressed outrage at the wife saying that she was a doctor, just like her husband was. I protested, 'Women can't be doctors. You're a nurse.' She calmly insisted otherwise. The adults all laughed at my adamance that she was not only mistaken, but really quite silly for being so ambitious. I really couldn't understand why she could not see how much better it was for her to be a nurse.

The roles of women in society were so much more enticing to me. Who would not want a starched nurse's uniform with a flattering hemline? Who would not want to be . . . nice? What was so appealing about being a surly, burly, hairy doctor? Ok sure, if he was dashingly handsome with mighty big hands and a tone I could trust, then he would always catch my eye, but that was as someone to be attracted to, not someone I thought any woman should seek to become! No, give me a secretarial job where I could wear a pencil skirt, a pussy-bow blouse, my hair in a chignon and provide an answer for everything. That, I could do. But the dream? My real childhood dream? To be a British Airways Air Stewardess.

You couldn't tell me anything when I began to fantasise about being a stewardess after our family trip to Jamaica in 1992. This impossibly glamorous woman took care of us, and looked like she loved doing so. Time slowed down for me when leaving the airport we saw her exit quickly with the cabin crew through the gates up ahead and the pilot made her laugh until her head fell back in ecstasy. I suddenly knew how to spell the word swoon. Nevertheless, at school, I was not stupid enough to relay this to anyone. I knew by now to lie and say that I wanted to be a pilot.

You forced me into lying. I knew I loved boys and I knew I was not one. I got beats at home. I got beats at school. I spoke my truth, clearly and all the way through nursery: I am a girl. From deep down under the ground, to way up high in the sky, I was sent here to fill the world with me. You told me the options for being human and I am telling you now:

- These are the girls I roll with.
- This is the body I want.
- This is who I love.
- This is the only way I want to be.

I buried these bullet points in my guts. Blood coated them in clots and the truth was ulcerous. I never forgot what they said. Acidic whispers disturbed my sleep and I would wake up unable to breathe. Just as the panic became unbearable and I was certain that this would be the way I would go – breathless and in limbo, not yet dead, but certainly far from really alive – I would gasp my way back into consciousness.

Still, I stayed loved. Mummy knew. She said she didn't, but she knew. I stole spritzes from her Kenzo perfume every morning while she showered. She allowed me though. 'It's like having a fifteen-year-old daughter,' she would tut towards me as the level of the liquid in the bottle dwindled down. Welp . . . Yeah! Briefly widened eyes, exhaling through my teeth before kissing my lips and finishing with a gentle shrug. A few years later, on a beach in Mexico she pointed out that I was growing boobs. She didn't intend to offend. This is a milestone that I now own with fond nostalgia. Mummy teasing me about my little nubs. Developing a bit later than other girls, but hey ho, at least they were here.

I've fallen in love time and time again and it is such an honour that the first man I loved was black. Deliciously black. Blue black I've heard some African-Americans call it. Our legs touched under the table in science and he made me lose my breath. The love remained pure because I needed it to be. He wanted me, close to him and in his home. He was not confused. He was scared but he was not confused. He told me his dreams as I leant on a brick wall. He kicked at the moss in the wet spring sunshine. He wanted to be a chef. I told him the path to realising that.

Twenty years later, I check into his social media and see him lift his son up with tender loving care. I hope he remembers that I believed in him and that I still do. I am glad I never told him that his light-skinned girlfriend told a group of us on the bus going through Wood Green, that he was too dark. I am glad I got the opportunity to disagree with her so vehemently, so early on in my career of survival. No matter how much self-hate spewed into the well of my knowledge, because I loved him, I could also love me.

'KUCHENGA! Why do you talk like a white girl for!?'
This was the winner for the most asked sentence of my secondary school experience. My answer to them was to sigh with

satisfaction and disdain. In my mind I would say, 'Well . . . I read a lot and . . . I wanna end up somewhere you're all too scared to go.'

I couldn't see how I could be both bad *and* bougie for too long, I grant you. Furthermore, as we are being frank, I couldn't be bothered to not date white guys. It felt convenient. I wanted to leapfrog my way into their world. I was thrilled that it pissed my father off too. It became one of my easiest acts of rebellion. I still speak to my black secondary school peers in quiet moments. I tell them, 'It further titillated me to be considered a traitor when there was more than enough evidence that I am actually an accomplished double agent. One of the best. I know their code and I know ours. I switch proficiently, but I know which one I prefer. I know you give me life. You think I could put my soul on ice like that? No. I will always love us for real. If we are being truthful, you allowed their dogmatic religion and biological determinism to stop you from seeing how infinite my love for you is. My name means "protector of the village" but you sent me into exile. Now I fly, but I am not happy to be rootless. Motherless. Fatherless. My once keenly felt sense of belonging has been ripped from my being.'

bell hooks says, 'Love is an action, never simply a feeling.' The young Philadelphia native Maurice 'Reese' Willoughby definitely thought this too. He took the gamble and chose to give his girlfriend Faith the delicious sensations that come with being loved out loud. Not just on road, but also online. He said he didn't care if she was passable. She was most definitely a woman to him, f**k what you all say. Boys took their phones out and burst the eardrums of those of us sensitive to hate, with hyena screeches that somehow did not shatter the glass doors of the fridges in the store they had stopped in to get some juice. Cyber-bullied into a death by suicide, whispers of abuse encircled his coffin, but they did not wake him. Did the glee of those who hounded him just evaporate when they found out how he died? What incriminating evidence was deleted in the days that followed?

Those boys have a strictly enforced policy. Girls like us can only be loved in secret, if at all. If you dare to try and love us outside of vampire hours, they will drain you of your success and make your world even smaller. You will be banished. Just like us.

First, a head. Then shoulders. Oh damn! Full torso? Is this lone soldier running towards us like Shaka Zulu with no army and no armour, but a shield made out of – *narrows eyes* – straightness? He says his name is Malik Yoba? Ok – so you all want to give him the Trans Cross of Ultimate Bravery for loving us openly on an open public stage? What a rough twenty-first century day, that it still takes so much to get so little? This one was a great candidate for the position of the one who could change opinions. His manhood was never in question. He identifies as straight and behaves accordingly. Nothing swishy about him. Finally, a man who could be respected. This African-American actor with a deep voice and broad shoulders elected himself to do the right thing and be finally open about his attraction to all women, including trans women.

Yet soon enough an allegation swirled around him too. How old were the girls in his past? His defence was sloppy. The 'he said, she said' dynamic of imbalanced gender relations was not mutated by the transness of his accuser. My mother taught me to give black men extra leeway. I did not then know why. She warned me of their petulance and I remembered that when I watched Malik Yoba stomp out of his interview with *The Root*. Doesn't he know that it takes more than an accusation to kill you?

On the streets of our cities, black trans girls are tossed out as if they are not beautiful and precious. In spite of our fortitude and our glory we are out here being murdered. Our killers follow the cues of transmisogynistic gate-keepers with an international reach, who cook up the acrimony in their own homes, offices and radio studios.

We all watched black trans director, producer and author Janet Mock wade in the waters of ignorance that submerges *The Breakfast Club* radio show. We held our breath in hope that her clearly expressed thoughts had got through to them. The following week they held up her ethereal face on her lauded second autobiography to be ridiculed by a rapper who will never become a household name. They spilt her tea and his response was, 'Well I would have to kill that nigga!' The radio hosts feigned dismay and shook their heads performing incredulity because *he* had gone too far. If you make black trans girls a target for male rage, and then suggest that any man who has been supposedly duped into finding us alluring is irrevocably emasculated, then you can be sure he will follow through, and murder his duplicitous transsexual emasculator. Still, I was astounded. For Janet Mock passes as cisgender to the point where she lived a stealth life, not telling anyone she was transgender for years. She has been married twice and is arrestingly beautiful, graces covers of magazines and flies to Paris to see the Valentino collection. She writes, produces, directs and helped birth the cultural phenomenon that is the show *POSE*, which has changed the landscape for black latinx trans inclusion in media forever. If she can be threatened with murder for the crime of existing, then what hope for the rest and the least of us. The homeless, the darker skinned, the sex workers and those of us who self-medicate with substances and survive in the world with disabilities and fat bodies and face assaults and traumas on the daily. Where is our black love?

Yet, I have been loved. There was a time. I belonged. My mother loved me. My father loved me. My community had hopes for me and told me I was bright and intelligent and that I had a bright future. The ritualistic and spiritual dimensions of my Venusian arrival caused too much commotion though. Thus, washed up on the shore with a wet wavy weave and shivering from a lack of shelter, love was snatched away, snuffed out and it left me abandoned and destitute. Still, I told myself, how dare I not survive?

Miss Major survived Attica prison. I can survive.

Frances Thompson survived the Memphis Riots. I can survive too.

Lucy Hicks Anderson survived the attempted destruction of her life. I can survive too.

My most recent ancestors are those whose voices are loudest. Naomi Hirsi, my Somali sis murdered in a hotel and mis-gendered in the courts and the papers. In the Old Bailey, I sat on a rough, hard green chair, my belongings signed into the back rooms of a travel agency down the road. With no phone to distract me, I could do nothing but stare at the glutinous milky face of her killer. He shook his head incredulously when the judge sentenced him to seven years, but he had the decency not to cry as he was sent down. He couldn't bring himself to look in my direction but he knew I was there. Grief grounded me in my purpose that day. I am glad he felt a black trans woman witness him face some kind of consequence. It wasn't enough. It never is.

I left the Old Bailey, glad that the rain had stopped and grateful that the sun was making its way through the skyscrapers way off up the road. I sat on a seat outside a coffee shop by St Paul's tube station and licked the cinnamon off the cream atop a chai latte. I finally cried down the phone to a Jamaican bus driver who had known her body as well as he now knew mine. Every time he came around, he would bring a carton of guava juice and a carton of mango juice. He fell asleep next to me under the crochet bedspread my mother had picked out on the roadside in Zimbabwe. Months later I would miss that bedspread because of the chill that crip-walked through my room when another Jamaican who made my face hot, told me that he had seen Stephen Lawrence on the bus a day or two before he was knifed down. I gave him space. Then in came an Angolan, optimistic and athletic whose lips kiss my thickness and who asks me questions that make me feel whole and full. He makes me laugh a lot.

Loving black men has transformed my politics. If I ruled the world I would free us all. I write to trans girls in prison and hope for the world that Angela Davis envisions for us. I want prisons to be obsolete. I want all drugs legalised. I want sex work to be decriminalised. I want poverty eradicated. Most of all I want an end to the violence I keep being told I have to get used to. Forgiveness did not teach me much of anything. It just gave me a lot of my time back. I embarked on a process of defining what justice is to me on my own terms. I got mine. Everyone deserves theirs.

My mother taught me to give black men extra leeway, and because I do, it has made me a better woman. I have gained a transcendental bliss from finding those who have been brave enough to love me back.

NAO

Neo Jessica Joshua, better known as Nao, is a provider of endless 'wonky funk' bops, best known as a Grammy and Mercury-nominated singer-songwriter and record producer from East London. But like so many women in our book, she is multi-talented, proving herself an excellent writer outside of music, too. As we brace ourselves for a post-Brexit Britain, her essay tackles what this might look like for black women, a group who are so often an afterthought in this country's political discourse. When talking about the many difficulties we face, she doesn't downplay them, but does what we as black women do best: find optimism amongst the exasperation.

We Were Made For These Times

When I was asked to write an essay on what the future holds for black women in an uncertain post-Brexit world it wasn't immediately obvious how to respond. I try to stay informed, but I'm no expert in politics or economics. I'm a musician.

Musicians are expressive and instinctive rather than predictive and analytical. I write about my experiences and my feelings, hoping that they resonate with people, maybe even resonate with society more broadly. I don't make predictions or grand statements. So, I decided to stick to what I know and tell you how *I feel* about the future. And it turned out, after thinking very hard about this, that feelings are important.

To consider a post-Brexit future, first I had to work out how I felt about our past and our present. What was life as a black British woman like *before* Brexit, Trump and the rise of the far right? Was it a utopian existence where prejudice didn't exist? Well, the short answer is no. It was confusing and often painful at times. It's not as if prejudice and inequality disappeared when Obama became the leader of the free world. The problem was systemic and generally hard to prove, and even if the evidence was available, was anyone willing to look at it?

As a woman of colour, I was being told the future was sorted, that I had just as many chances as everyone else in life. With free movement across twenty-eight different countries and freedom to speak out on social media there were no walls (and no talk of walls in Mexico). But it didn't *feel* like that. When I found myself – as the only black person in the shop – being followed around by suspicious staff, when I saw my brown and black-skinned friends picked up by police for stop-and-search, or pulled out of airport queues by security, it didn't *feel* like we had prejudice nailed. When I saw women of colour being ignored by the media, paid less than their male counterparts and almost entirely absent from the upper echelons of business, that didn't *feel* like equality. But Obama was in office and diversity was the buzz word and one might have believed that the world was heading in the right direction.

It's not as if my life was bad back then. I was working as a professional musician, but I struggled with confidence and, as you may have heard me say before, I never thought that becoming an artist, touring and releasing music across the world was a possibility for me as there were only a small handful of black artists in the UK who had previously done so. I think other young black and minority ethnic people felt the same way about jobs at the top of their industries. We believed those jobs were for a different type of person.

And then the 2016 Referendum happened. Its immediate aftermath was as bad as could be expected, especially for BME women. Incidents of racism increased, poisonous colonial nonsense started seeping into the right-wing press and people previously only able to whisper in pubs found the courage to share their views on social media. UKIP – with the added voice of the EDL – seized 12 per cent of the vote in the 2017 election and, all of a sudden, it seemed as though we were heading back to the 1970s.

Then, in 2018, came The Windrush Scandal. It felt like the final blow to Britain as a progressive, liberal nation. What had previously been merely the bickering of the political elite became the nation's burning desire to make Britain great again: to go back to the good old days when England still colonised 25 per cent of the world, before foreigners ruined everything and everyone could buy a house for a hundred pounds.

Against this backdrop it would be right to be pretty pessimistic about the future. Yet despite it all, I still feel that there is cause for hope. As many of us know from our own lives, things often get worse before they get better. And in the midst of all the negativity of these recent years, I have seen – and I'm still seeing – something beautiful arising in direct response: the power of the youth.

Young people are passionately taking up the challenge of resistance, not just in Britain but across the world. Teenagers and young adults have stepped up to lead some of the world's biggest conversations. And finding themselves faced with this huge question about the future of their country, young British people – particularly BME people – have engaged more with politics than at any other time in history. Record numbers of young people had registered to vote in the upcoming election in 2019, and 1 in 5 new voters were BME (more than the national average). People have marched, people have written, people have used social media in innovative ways. In the world of British music, inspirational figures like Stormzy, Dave, Little Simz, Idles and slowthai (to name a few) have emerged, and are creating modern-day protest music.

I myself – having previously only sung – have been inspired to speak. I've felt empowered to join the debate and have spoken to young people at Oxford University, Cambridge University, *Elle Weekender*, Blackgirlfest, *gal-dem* and The Southbank. I *feel* we are creating space and engaging in our futures as a collective more now than ever before. In finding my voice I've sought out others who are engaging on a huge range of important topics – not just in Britain but across the world – and I feel so hopeful about the next generation.

I found Ash Sakar, a 26-year-old journalist who is re-inventing and re-invigorating British politics, taking on men in high places, head to head – and winning. I found Artemisa Xakriabá, a proud woman of colour fighting against climate change, defending the earth and its indigenous people. I found Elijah Walters-Othman, a 17-year-old working-class black man whose speech at the UK Youth Parliament debate was met with a standing ovation. I found Liv Little, writer, businesswoman and editor of *gal-dem* who at 25 years old is changing the face of UK publishing. And I found Fahma Mohamed who recently became the youngest ever recipient of a doctorate from Bristol University at 19 for her work against FGM. This is just to name a few of a generation who have fought back and, in that fight, are reaching new heights.

So . . . and here comes the clickbait headline . . . was . . . the Brexit referendum . . . a . . . good thing? Did we actually *need* to have a debate about the future of Britain and sort a few things out? Was the 'it's all fine, don't worry yourself about it' status quo holding us back? Although it's sometimes hard to see, I believe that seeds of good have being sown these last few years and there is hope for the future, there is light at the end of the tunnel. I believe we have found a new political activism and energised our young people. We've found a progressive global cause that we can unite behind. And in that unity we are finding strength and joy.

For sure, there are still serious issues with prejudice and inequality but it seems like now we're at least talking about these issues, and they're no longer being swept under the rug. And in talking about them I feel like we are getting somewhere slowly. In education, publishing, advertising, technology, fashion and beauty there are serious conversations – not just box-ticking – beginning to happen and chinks of light are showing through the clouds.

There is still much to do and we must be vigilant, united and strong, but I am excited to believe that the next generation can at least begin to dream about a different, better, more equal future.

PAULA AKPAN

Paula is a journalist and co-founder of Black Girl Fest, an arts and culture festival celebrating Black women and non-binary people. We particularly admire how the festival has created a platform where black girls can take up space and be unapologetically themselves and loud.

A sociology graduate from the University of Nottingham, Paula's writing focuses on race, queerness and social politics. In her essay, Paula explores the allure of 'secure your bag' politics, as well as its dangers: a timely topic given the rise of the influence industry and the age of 'woke' brands. She writes brilliantly about the tensions that can arise when trying to navigate the path between being your authentic self and interrogating any brands you choose to work with.

The Quandary
of Securing the Bag

The last few years have been a whirlwind for me. Alongside the creation of a multidisciplinary festival solely dedicated to the celebration and platforming of Black women and girls, I have also made big strides in my work as a journalist, facilitator and speaker. I've written for publications I religiously pored over when I was younger and taken up space on stages that the teenage Paula would've balked at. I've been welcomed into rooms alongside Black women I've long admired and I can often be found very subtly pinching myself in a corner of the room after coming into contact with them. It's been a heady journey that has offered very little time and room for acclimatisation to the feeling of being suddenly very visible and seen.

Increased visibility tends to bring with it some form of clout, whether it's in the shape of followers, more weight being given to your opinions or, potentially, brands becoming interested in you. Over the last five years, I've found myself working with brands and organisations whose products and services I grew up coveting; brands that had once seemed faceless and abstract are now wanting to align themselves with my work.

But when that work is born out of a community focus – whether creating a cultural event, writing to raise awareness of specific issues and histories, creating collectives and our own institutions to tackle a particular need – how do we ensure that our initial causes and messages are not diluted by an influx of opportunities? Is there a way that we can make sure that we continue building our culturally important contributions and hold onto our ethos, whilst also fully exploring the possibility of collaborating with other organisations? If you're someone like me, who is not in a full-time, 9 to 5 salaried position, these questions become even more urgent as ever-looming bills and rent enter the equation.

Going freelance for the first time a year ago was a baptism by fire for me. I made the, in retrospect, unwise decision to pack in my job just before Christmas (presents for my family ended up being extremely imaginative and crafty). However, in spite of the timing, it felt like a necessary next step. I had gotten a taste for journalism during my time at university and the allure of being able to centre issues, communities and experiences that mattered to me became all too tempting. I also wanted to have time to work on the projects and opportunities that were being offered to me regularly, without having to fit them into my weekends or take time off in order to pursue them. While it was a huge leap, with plenty of room for error, going freelance meant that I would no longer be working on someone else's dream or project while trying to fit the organisation of mine into rushed lunchtime phone calls and post-work meetings.

Without the security of a guaranteed monthly salary, all my income and spending went under the microscope – did I really need that new book to add to my growing pile of unread books? (It turns out, yes, yes I did.) Could I walk instead of taking the bus? (A far more begrudging yes.) I stepped up the pace of my work, with pitch ideas flying from my fingers while I continued to build my profile as a public speaker.

The panic would often catch up with me in the evenings: I'd be trying to switch off for the night and then would suddenly be waylaid by the thought of where on earth that huge chunk of rent money was going to come from and which dinners and events I'd have to cancel in the upcoming week to hold onto those pennies.

Thanks to the circles I'm a part of, there's some solace in knowing that I'm not the only one trying to make sense of the world of self-employment. Social media platforms have given me access to writing and speaking opportunities, but they have also revealed to me other people's struggles with being offered exposure as payment, as well as offering useful resources for how to ensure being paid on time and navigate late fees. These platforms are also where I first came across the idea of 'securing the bag'.

Defined as 'obtaining financial security', securing the bag tends to evoke imagery of finessing, hustling and taking advantage of a situation. Having been popularised by celebrities such as Cardi B, it is normally used in reference to entrepreneurship, however there are also articles online that explore how to secure the bag while in a 9 to 5 job, through setting goals for desired pay and investing in professional certifications. While the turn of phrase is often used ironically, it stems from the concept of ensuring that the value of one's work, services or brand is reflected in monetary gain, particularly for Black creatives and freelancers.

Even when bag securing is not explicitly referred to, the running thread of being paid at least proportionately for your time and worth can be seen through the rise of support initiatives for start-up founders, campaigners and freelancers. These can come in the form of newsletters packed with tips for chasing emails, round-ups of the latest job opportunities, and WhatsApp groups made with the purpose of transparently sharing fees for speaking engagements. It's also there in publicly calling out organisations for poor practice, or even reminding fellow creatives to up their fees in anticipation of months like Black History Month or Pride Month, when brands and corporations attempt to prove their support for these communities – especially when that support has previously been lacking.

When it comes to brands, from beauty to tech, Black women have long been an afterthought. From limited product ranges to marketing and promotional campaigns that are questionable at best, and downright racist at worst, many of us share the experiences of having spending power and yet, never being catered to, never being considered and never seeing ourselves in the decision-making roles of these brands. 'For a long time, Black women were seen as a downmarket demographic, or else not seen at all,' highlights journalist Siham Ali during her exploration of the hostility of the beauty industry to Black women for Foundry Fox.[1]

Because marketers have never considered the true collective power of the 'Black pound', they have always struggled to create effective strategies to attract it. Black women are relegated to being a 'hard to reach community' simply because appropriate research often hasn't been done, messaging rings hollow and is devoid of a real understanding of our experiences. And it doesn't just stop at brands and corporations with products and services to sell. Mental health trusts, charities and civic institutions also fail to connect with Black women service users in the right ways, with specific issues lost within a one-size-fits-all approach towards women's needs. Having been let down by organisations and their strategies on multiple occasions, it's no wonder we have become distrustful and cynical towards tired and half-baked marketing ploys.

As a result, these organisations are now looking to a range of Black women influencers to help them bridge the gap, through sponsored posts, campaigns or gifting (providing influencers with free products, services and experiences, often in exchange for sharing on their social media platforms): from the macro-influencers (with between 100,000 and a million followers gained through vlogging and podcasting platforms), to micro-influencers (1,000 to 100,000 followers) who tend to be experts on one particular area, to ambassadors who promote and advocate on behalf of an organisation.

In the last couple of years, however, there has been another addition to the influencer marketing world: the cultural influencer. As Lucy Odigie-Turley notes for *The Opportunity Agenda*, these types of influencers move beyond corporate promotion and instead tend to be 'high-profile individuals who are using their visibility to engage with critical social issues'.[2] People like Tarana Burke, the founder of the awareness-raising #MeToo movement, Colin Kaepernick, the former American quarterback who knelt during the national anthem in protest of police brutality, and Akala, rapper, author and political activist, did not necessarily seek out the influence they now wield, but through online platforms they have been able to spark conversations around a number of critical issues.

The quandary for Black creatives and freelancers can arise when they become attractive to organisations looking to align themselves more with people who have strong messages, well-connected networks and demonstrably strong ties with their communities. These creatives offer something that an influencer with hundreds of thousands of followers can never guarantee: authenticity. While the output of commercial influencers is often characterised as superficial and shallow, the work of writers, journalists and cultural producers stands in stark contrast and is perceived as adding more value to the world – especially if their work hones in on a community need. But as our identities as Black women become more desirable to brands and organisations, what does it mean when we choose to work with them? How does that affect the work we do? And how does it affect the way we carry ourselves online?

The commodification of self, according to Joseph E. Davis, a Research Associate Professor of Sociology at the University of Virginia, can be defined as '[involving] the reorganisation of our personal lives and relationships on the model of market relationships. This adaptation is well illustrated by the recent practice of "personal branding", a strategy of cultivating a name and image of ourselves that we manipulate for economic gain.'[3] He notes that 'self-branding as self-empowerment' advocates, such as authors of self-help book *Brand Yourself*, David Andrusia and Rick Haskins, insist that 'if people treat themselves as a product, then they can beat the corporate world at its own game, turning the power of branding around to personal advantage'. Once again, we're told that there is a situation to take advantage of and a bag to be secured.

In an article in the *Guardian*, writer Allegra Hobbs took a look at the way we sell ourselves on social media: in particular, authors and journalists who are nowadays not too dissimilar from lifestyle celebrities. She notes that to be a writer today is 'to make yourself a product for public consumption on the internet, to project an appealing image that contextualises the actual writing. The women – and they are mostly women – who are most heralded in the media industry today are extremely online, starring in photoshoots and documenting their skincare routines and eating habits as much as discussing their process.' The once clear line between the creative and the social media influencer has become blurred, especially when 'personal branding' comes into play.[4]

Marketing and communications expert Reyna Matthes defines this form of branding as 'an extension of the "self-improvement for success" phenomenon', however, she notes that what sets it apart is the focus on self-packaging: 'At its best, personal branding is about building your identity capital. This means understanding and building on the individual gifts and assets that you bring to your situation . . . someone with strong identity capital shapes the elements of their identity to form a meaningful and coherent whole. They gain respect and influence because of who they are/ what they do.'

'Model of market relationships', 'public consumption' and 'capital' are all terms that some of us may remember from business studies and economics back in school, and yet this is the language we now use to try to understand the value and worth of an individual's contributions. For me, this feels particularly at odds with the aims of someone working to platform and advance community initiatives. It's even more of a striking contrast when we consider the historic subjugation of Black women and the ways that we are still reminded of how the world ranks us, from the concrete ceiling for Black women in the workplace to the minefield that is the world of dating. This new-found cultural capital is unfamiliar and many of us are treating it with suspicion, considering that we're still living many of these experiences of subjugation.

But for now, Black womanhood is in. Many brands aren't actively including Black women in their campaigns out of the goodness of their hearts, however. It is because they have finally become aware of our previously untapped spending power – in part because of the monumental rise of names like Rihanna's Fenty Beauty, a brand that has always sought to keep Black women at the centre of the conversation rather than at the margins. In Siham Ali's Foundry Fox report she also notes that online platforms have elevated our voices in a way that hasn't existed before. 'The rise of social media platforms like Twitter has given a voice to those who have difficulty being heard,' she writes. 'It has allowed us to make the [beauty] industry see Black women as active consumers, rather than idle spectators.' As consumers, we've never before witnessed so much choice or so many efforts to try to engage us. As a result, visible Black women creatives now find themselves navigating the relatively unexplored territory of holding relative influence with both brands and their communities, simultaneously.

So what does this mean for us? For example, does any message you share become tainted when it comes in the form of sponsored content? Does it suggest that all creatives are up for sale when it's the right price? How do you hold onto your authenticity when you're expected to curate, package and present bits of yourself? These are just a few of the many questions that have been bouncing around my head as my journalism and projects have boosted my profile. And because this is such a new cultural phenomenon, I'm yet to find the answers I'm looking for. What I do know, however, is that the decisions I make and the brands and people I choose to work with have an impact outside of my immediate bubble: they reflect on my projects and by extension, the communities I'm a part of.

Over the last couple of years, I have worked with brands on projects I'm immensely proud of, because I felt like they provided my communities with something important, whether it was access to resources that aren't ordinarily easy to come by, or facilitating important conversations on a big stage. But I've also worked on freelance projects with organisations that, on reflection, I'm pretty embarrassed about. In those instances, I lost my way attempting to weave the brand's key messages with the aim of celebrating my communities fully. These experiences have led me to have serious conversations with myself about the projects I choose to undertake going forward, interrogating whether they are offering something of value, particularly to Black women, Black girls and Black LGBTQ+ folk.

As a freelance writer, I've been privy to the dark underbelly of my profession. In a field where 94 per cent of journalists are white, it's certainly no walk in the park for Black women journalists. I've watched gatekeepers maintain influence through nepotism, while proudly feminist media publications have gone into administration, leaving staff writers and their freelancers floundering with thousands of pounds owed. I've also observed the way that accountability tends to be shirked by many of the journalists who work at tabloids known for peddling bigoted and dangerous views, often citing that they can't ignore what editors tell them to write.

Watching my counterparts refuse to take responsibility for the roles they play in putting out stories that can be actively harmful has in some ways made me double down on the type of journalist I want to be. With my writing, I try to focus on the people and topics that are crucial to the communities I'm a part of, as a Black lesbian woman, but also the communities I'm not a part of but whose stories I'm in a position to help platform. I've spoken to a stripper collective about the current working conditions for sex workers in the UK and their goals, talked to a number of LGBTQ+ folk about why they haven't 'come out' and the implications of that, and I've discussed the importance of documenting the experiences of Black women in the UK with historians and activists like author, and former British Black Panther, Beverley Bryan, and the UK's first Black woman book publisher, Margaret Busby: women whose work has been formative in my understanding of my history and the histories of Black women who have gone before me.

My work often centres around interviews and people-led narratives and I believe that this has played a significant part in my understanding of the matters close to the hearts of my communities. I'm able to leverage my position and access in a way that can amplify voices long deemed too disruptive, while continuing to educate myself, often on issues I thought I had a good understanding of, but, as it turned out, I had barely scratched the surface.

Utilising journalism as a way to bring in others has been foundational to the way I can use other platforms I hold influence over, rather than lean into the temptation of staying focused on securing the bag. There's certainly an appeal when it comes to adding reputable names to a roster of brands you've worked with, especially when there's the unforgiving rent to meet and it feels like every opportunity could be that next career-defining moment, putting you in front of a new audience and providing you with further reach. However, in the same way that being recognised for work you've done within your community can elevate your visibility, it's also abundantly clear when someone no longer seems to be in touch with matters that are critical to that same community.

When your work, your opinions and your voice no longer function to amplify the voices and experiences of the people you set out to serve, but rather operate solely as a vessel for organisations to transmit their messaging, surely it's time to stop and examine your own motives, and to ask who, in the end, really benefits?

References

1 'The beauty industry: a hostile foreign place for black women?', (7 June 2018) <http://foundryfox.com/4633/beauty-hostile-to-Black-women/#.xGdkBtXSv4>

2 'More Than Just a Fad: The Power of the Cultural Influencer', (14 March 2019) <https://www.opportunityagenda.org/explore/insights/more-just-fad-power-cultural-influencer>

3 'The Commodification of Self' from *The Hedgehog Review*, 5.2 (Summer 2003) <https://hedgehogreview.com/issues/the-commodification-of-everything/articles/the-commodification-of-self>

4 Allegra Hobbs, 'The journalist as influencer: how we sell ourselves on social media', *Guardian*, (21 October 2019) <https://www.theguardian.com/media/2019/oct/20/caroline-calloway-writers-journalists-social-media-influencers

PHOEBE PARKE

Phoebe is currently a social media editor and journalist at *Grazia UK* as well as a former CNN journalist. She and Yomi ended up connecting several years later than they probably should have: Phoebe was an undergraduate at Warwick university at the same time as Yomi (and Liz) and they had near identical routes into journalism, often interning at the same magazines and news-papers within a few weeks of each other. We are lucky to now be able to count Phoebe as a friend. Here, Phoebe writes about mixed race identity, focusing on the importance of language and labels.

The Meghan Markle Effect Made Mixed Race Identity a Hot Topic, But Are We Any Further Forward?

The date was Sunday, 27 November 2016 and a mixed-race actress from Los Angeles, California had just been confirmed as Prince Harry's girlfriend. The next day, the newsroom I was working in was still reeling from the announcement, buzzing with the excitement that always comes with breaking news. For my part, I found myself experiencing a feeling of immense pride, but also of overwhelming dread, which rose up from the pit of my stomach and into my throat.

The pride came from seeing someone who looked like me accepted by the British royal family – something I hadn't thought I'd ever see in my lifetime. We were about to have a mixed-race duchess, and even I couldn't have imagined the impact this would have.

The dread came from knowing what the reaction from some members of the British public would be: I imagined a pervasive wind of racism wafting towards her from newspaper headlines, Instagram comments and conversations on daytime talk shows. In reality it was more like a hurricane, sweeping along with it misogynoir, ignorance and out and out racism.

Even though the announcement had absolutely nothing to do with me, I suddenly felt as though a piercing spotlight had been shone on my mixed-race identity, and I braced myself for the questions that would surely come.

And boy did they come. Colleagues asked me about the texture of Meghan's hair and told me they hoped she'd have it curly for the wedding; radio stations contacted me to ask how I felt about Danny Baker posting a racist monkey cartoon with a caption about the royal baby, and I was called on to explain which terminology was socially acceptable when describing Meghan's ethnicity, and why.

Suddenly mixed-race identity was centre stage, and people couldn't stop talking about it.

The Power of the Meghan Markle Effect

'The Meghan Markle Effect' is a phrase used to describe the phenomenon of people buying items as soon as the Duchess of Sussex wears them, causing them to sell out. The public has always been obsessed with what celebrities wear, rushing out to buy the same pieces or cheaper high street copies, but in the case of Meghan – and of her sister-in-law Kate – it's the element of surprise that creates the hysteria.

Here's why: royals can't accept gifts, which means they have to return any bags, shoes or clothes sent to them, so it's often a complete surprise when a brand sees one of their items being worn by a member of the royal family, and sometimes they aren't at all prepared.

There are websites solely dedicated to identifying what Meghan and Kate are wearing, finding the link to buy it, and sharing it with their thousands of followers. Designers are given no advance warning that one of their items is suddenly going to be thrust into the limelight, and so sometimes websites crash, items sell out in seconds because they aren't well-stocked and in some cases whole businesses end up going under, unable to cope with the sheer number of customers coming their way so unexpectedly.

One such example is the brand Issa, which Kate Middleton wore for her engagement announcement in 2010. As Kate stood proudly next to Prince William in a royal blue wrap dress, images of the couple were being sent around the world, and it wasn't long before the brand was identified, its website found and within minutes the dress was sold out.

What Kate might not have realised is that wearing the dress unwittingly brought Issa to the verge of financial crisis, founder Daniella Helayel told the *Daily Mail* in 2016.[1] When the dress was identified, sales doubled overnight, the bank wouldn't provide credit, and the factory needed to be paid, and so the brand ultimately shut down. Helayel went on to create another successful fashion line called Dhela, but this is still a powerful reminder of how much influence Kate and Meghan wield.

'The Meghan Markle Effect' hasn't led to the closure of any businesses that we know of yet, but from the Strathberry crossbody bag that sold out and had a 3,000 person waiting list after Meghan wore it in Edinburgh, to the Parosh dress she chose for her engagement interview that you still can't buy for love nor money, and even the purple Officeworks folder Meghan used to cover her baby bump as she arrived in Sydney on her royal tour in 2018, Meghan can make pretty much anything she wears, or holds, sell out.

During Meghan and Harry's tour of southern Africa in 2019, global fashion search engine Lyst reported that searches for Staud dresses had soared by 625 per cent after Meghan wore the brand's 'Millie Dress'; searches for the Club Monaco dress she wore on day two were up 570 per cent, and her black Everlane jumpsuit appearance increased searches for 'black jumpsuits' by 384 per cent.

It was reported that surgeons were expected to see a huge uptake in bunion surgery after the world got a glimpse of what may or may not have been a small scar on the Duchess's feet during her 2018 royal tour, when she went barefoot while participating in a welcome ceremony in New Zealand.

But it's not just Meghan's style that has taken centre stage, as Meghan has become more famous, so conversations around mixed-race identity have become more frequent – although not necessarily more eloquent or better informed.

A Note on Privilege

It's time for an acknowledgement of privilege before we go any further. Being mixed race in the UK, and many other countries, brings with it a healthy dollop of privilege. The obnoxious and toxic laws of colourism dictate that the lighter your skin the more desirable you are, the less threatening you seem, the less likely you are to be a victim of racism.

While I'll share some of my experiences as a mixed-race woman in this essay, they, quite literally, pale in comparison to the experiences of black women in Britain and beyond, and the constant ignorant barrage of life-threatening racism and misogynoir they endure.

How the Public Talks About Meghan's Mixed-Race Identity

I first heard the name Meghan Markle when a boyfriend at the time told me there was an actress he fancied who looked like me in a legal drama he was watching on Netflix. Being the jealous girlfriend that I was, I immediately started watching *Suits*, and while the only things Rachel Zane and I had in common were approximate skin tone, hair colour and a penchant for pencil skirts, a rare comment on race made me an instant fan of her character. It was during an exchange between Rachel and colleague Mike, who is astonished to learn that Rachel's father is black. Rachel responds by asking whether Mike thought that she was simply sporting a year-round tan. The clumsy TV moment hit close to home.

I too have had to 'come out' as mixed race to white colleagues, and just like Rachel Zane I found the experience completely baffling. The *Suits* episode dramatised an all-too-common lack of understanding of mixed-race identity. In my experience we're either being asked where we're from as soon as we walk in the door – with pictures of our parents demanded as immediate proof of ethnicity – or, if we're 'white passing' – a term I'll use here for ease but I've never been comfortable with – we're assumed to be white until further notice.

While she was still an actress in *Suits*, Meghan wrote about her experience as a self-identifying mixed-race woman in an article for *Elle*, recounting how tired she was of being asked where she is from.[2]

'What are you?' A question I get asked every week of my life, often every day. 'Well,' I say, as I begin the verbal dance I know all too well. 'I'm an actress, a writer, the Editor-in-Chief of my lifestyle brand The Tig, a pretty good cook and a firm believer in handwritten notes.' A mouthful, yes, but one that I feel paints a pretty solid picture of who I am. But here's what happens: they smile and nod politely, maybe even chuckle, before getting to their point, 'Right, but what are you? Where are your parents from?' I knew it was coming, I always do. While I could say Pennsylvania and Ohio, and continue this proverbial two-step, I instead give them what they're after: 'My dad is Caucasian and my mom is African-American. I'm half black and half white.'

If Meghan was already exasperated with conversations about her mixed-race identity in this 2015 essay, we can only imagine how she feels now, having endured years of both coded and blatant racism from many – although not all – British media outlets. It's telling, and incredibly disappointing that Harry's announcement confirming Meghan as his girlfriend ended up being almost entirely about the racist comments she had already received, claiming Meghan had been 'subject to a wave of abuse and harassment'.

'Some of this has been very public,' he wrote. 'The smear on the front page of a national newspaper; the racial undertones of comment pieces; and the outright sexism and racism of social media trolls and web article comments. Some of it has been hidden from the public – the nightly legal battles to keep defamatory stories out of papers; her mother having to struggle past photographers in order to get to her front door; the attempts of reporters and photographers to gain illegal entry to her home and the calls to police that followed; the substantial bribes offered by papers to her ex-boyfriend; the bombardment of nearly every friend, co-worker, and loved one in her life.'

The statement from Harry sent shockwaves through the press, it was absolutely unprecedented for a member of the royal family to issue a statement so emotional, so bold and so wholeheartedly clear in its opposition to racism.

Two years later, Meghan and Harry got married – and as I read some of the social media comments that day, it was clear to me that people really thought this wedding somehow hailed the end of the UK's racial divide. They commented on how 'modern' the wedding was, how 'diverse' the ceremony, how this was such 'a huge step' for the royal family. And while everyone was basking in the woke glow of the royal wedding, telling me how much they loved the 'black preacher', gospel choir and Meghan's 'squad' rolling up to St George's Chapel, I was going around bursting everyone's self-righteous balloons with my push pin of reality saying, 'Stop calling her modern!'

I decided to take a look back at Kate and William's wedding in 2011 for comparison, and I found that it was a surprisingly similar event. Both wedding dresses had been designed by British designers and had long sleeves with flower-embroidered veils, both brides wore Welsh-gold wedding bands and engagement rings with stones from Princess Diana's collection, both wore tiaras borrowed from the Queen, both their bouquets contained a sprig of myrtle – a royal tradition dating back to Queen Victoria's wedding.

Both brides had young children as their bridesmaids and page-boys; the Queen wore a hat designed by Angela Kelly on both occasions; guests Victoria Beckham, David Beckham and Elton John were present at both weddings.

Both newly-wed couples posed holding hands as they exited the church for the crowds – resulting in strikingly similar pictures – both couples rode in carriages after the wedding before both brides changed into floor-length white reception dresses.

So what was so modern about Meghan and Harry's wedding? Could it have something to do with the fact that they are an inter-racial couple?

But Being Mixed Race Is Nothing New

'Mixed-race relationships are no longer an exotic rarity but the new normal', a *Daily Telegraph* headline read in November 2017, in response to Meghan and Harry's engagement.

Not quite. Scholars have been documenting interracial relationships in Britain since at least 1578, according to research by Chamion Caballero and Peter J. Aspinall. They quote Captain George Best who commented that he had 'seen an Ethiopian as black as coal brought to England, who taking a fair English woman to wife, begat a son in all respects as black as the father'.

The book, *Mixed Race Britain in The Twentieth Century* goes on to explore how common interracial relationships continued to be in Britain: 'the author Philip Thicknesse (1778) complained that in "every country town, nay, in almost every village are to be seen a little race of mulattoes, mischievous as monkeys, and infinitely more dangerous."'[3]

And while everyone was declaring that Meghan Markle was to be Britain's first black royal, they conveniently forgot about

Princess Sophia Charlotte of Mecklenburg-Strelitz who, according to some historians, was of African and Portuguese descent, and became the first black royal when she married King George III in 1761.

Historians have also noted that, during slavery in the US, the mixed-race children of white male slave owners and black female slaves were referred to as 'children of the plantation' and born into slavery. They were classified as 'mulatto' and because of the 'one drop rule' – the concept that if you have any black heritage at all then you are black – they could never be part of white society and weren't acknowledged by their white fathers.

Over the decades, a number of terms for mixed-race people have been used, from 'half-caste' to 'mulatto' and 'half and half', and the fact that these are now all seen as derogatory provides some insight into how attitudes towards mixed-race people have changed over time.

Clumsy Labels and Why I Cling to Mine

And so, we've inherited a bunch of clumsy labels to describe ourselves, and like Meghan who referred to herself as a 'proud mixed-race woman' in the *Elle* essay mentioned above, I label myself as mixed race. Biracial and dual heritage are becoming more popular alternatives, but sound so American to my British ears. As a teenager I got used to ticking the 'other' box on forms, before it was replaced by some more nuanced offerings. Now, whenever I tick the more specific 'mixed: white and black Caribbean' box, I wonder how important these labels really are.

A label can be useful in some ways: as a child it helped me identify myself and understand where I had 'come from'. My mother is black, born in Jamaica; my father is white, born in England, and I was a mix of the two – my skin colour kind of halfway between the two, hair texture sort of a mix of the two. Understood.

At school my first nickname was 'confused.com', I was told I was the product of jungle fever (something I didn't understand the meaning of until much later, but it brought tears to my eyes nonetheless) and fetishised as I grew older because of the colour of my skin. I remember being chatted up by guys who got my attention with calls of 'yo lighty' from across the road as I left Tiger Tiger in Croydon at the early hours of the morning to get the bus back home.

I found security in the label of 'mixed race', mainly because no one was likely to tell me that I didn't belong in that category. Growing up – and even sometimes now – I was jokingly told that I needed to embrace my 'black side' when I came up short on some arbitrary metric such as fondness for rice and peas (it's the kidney beans, I'm just not into them). And at school I couldn't always relate to my white classmates who bonded over shows I wasn't allowed to watch and hairstyles I could never hope to replicate. I've never taken any of this too seriously, and I realise that being confused about my identity wasn't just because of my ethnicity – it was a teenage thing. Nonetheless I still cling to my mixed-race label because it feels like a crude but safe rubber ring.

We're All Talking About Mixed-Race Identity, But Are We Any Further Forward?

Google news data shows that articles published containing the words 'mixed race' have tripled since 2015. Some are linked to Meghan Markle, and others just use her as a news hook for a deeper conversation. In recent years I have found myself, alongside other journalists of colour, frequently being asked to talk about mixed-race identity and Meghan Markle. But are these conversations, think pieces and panel discussions actually becoming more nuanced?

The reality is that some are and some aren't. When you provide a platform for conversations about ethnicity and identity you provide a platform for all kinds of opinions: some you agree with, and others you won't. But, even when they're not, an increase in people of colour's opinions being heard on matters of ethnicity cannot be a bad thing.

Unfortunately, however, the number of nuanced conversations about mixed-race identity is no match for the number of people being prejudiced and racist.

Meghan Markle is making her voice heard in the work she does as the Duchess of Sussex and is unapologetic about including people of colour in places of prominence in that work. When she guest-edited *Vogue*, over half of the 'Forces for Change' stars she put on the front cover were people of colour; she chose a dress by mixed-race designer Grace Wales Bonner at a time when all the eyes in the world were on her (for her first public appearance with baby Archie) and she selected several models of colour when shooting images for her Smart Works collection.

After these inclusions there was a noticeable increase in the backlash against her by people who might not consider themselves racist, but who continue to use coded language when talking about her. She's a 'diva', 'social climber' and the 'difficult Duchess'. These comments reached fever pitch after Meghan and Harry announced their step back from duties as senior royals, and while it was presented as joint decision, the vast majority of the backlash was directed at Meghan. As a helpful overview, *BuzzFeed* published an article looking at twenty headlines and how they treated Kate Middleton and Meghan Markle, suggesting this might be one of the reasons the Sussex family decided to cut off royal reporters. Where Kate was praised for holding her baby bump, Meghan was accused of being vain. Kate's love of avocados was hailed as a morning sickness cure, where Meghan's penchant for the fruit was linked to human rights abuses. Meghan was berated for missing Christmas with the royals, but Kate often spends her festive season with her parents.

There is an overarching impression I get when reading articles, looking at Instagram comments and overhearing conversations about Meghan: that she has ideas above her station. How dare this divorced, American, mixed-race thirty-something woman not only succeed in her acting and blogging career, but then think herself worthy of marrying into what is arguably the most powerful family in the UK?

Three years after Harry's statement to the press about racism, it's clear matters have only got worse. Another statement issued by the Duke of Sussex on 1 October 2019 declared that he was taking legal action against a tabloid newspaper, stating, 'Unfortunately, my wife has become one of the latest victims of a British tabloid press that wages campaigns against individuals with no thought to the consequences – a ruthless campaign that has escalated over the past year, throughout her pregnancy and while raising our newborn son.'

Meghan Markle Has Opened a Door

Meghan Markle's rise to fame has brought mixed-race identity into the glare of the spotlight, dragging with it some of the most heinous racist opinions that previously lurked in the shadows.

Whatever our views on Meghan Markle, the royal family and the British media, we now find ourselves in an unprecedented moment in which identity and ethnicity are being spoken about more frequently. While we might not all be comfortable defending our lived experiences to people who have made a career by playing 'devil's advocate', it's important that we add our authentic voices to the dialogue about women of colour and mixed-race identity, because these conversations are going to happen, with or without us.

It is my hope that in our own ways, through mediums that safeguard our mental health, ways that feel right to us, ways that we are proud of and ways that we are adequately paid for, we feel confident enough to add our own voices to the discussion being had about our identities.

References

1 https://www.dailymail.co.uk/home/you/article-4228010/Life-Kate-Effect-Issa-Helayel.html#ixzz4ZTlG7g6A
2 https://www.elle.com/uk/life-and-culture/news/a26855/more-than-an-other/
3 Caballero, C. & Aspinall, P. J. *Mixed Race Britain in The Twentieth Century* (Pan Macmillan: 2018)

PRINCESS PEACE

In 2017, Yomi was asked to speak at LSE's annual Black Ascent conference, on the theme 'The True Power of the Black Pound'. It was a wonderful and thought-provoking event, but the most memorable part of the evening was the closing performance by poet Princess Ashilokun, also known as Princess Peace. She was still a student at Oxford when she performed, but had the skill of a seasoned pro twice her age and experience. We had already been discussing the idea of curating a *Slay In Your Lane* anthology, and mentally confirmed her as our first contributor before we'd even pitched the book to publishers. Her essay is a reflection on her dual identity as a British-Nigerian woman and living 'loud and proud as Lagos traffic' in a world that so often seeks to silence us.

As Loud as Lagos Traffic

Growing up as a young Black-British Nigerian girl in the UK, my mother would ask me to scratch off the back of numerous calling cards to Nigeria. I'd often find myself scraping off the thin silvery-black coating that gathered under my fingernails, leaving little traces on her phone as I punched the digits into her small black Nokia. I endured many a long conversation with aunties and uncles whose voices I didn't always recognise, and yet who were adamant that they had known me since I was a foetus. In my pre-teens, spending five minutes on the phone felt like five decades. I was a young girl with important business affairs to tend to, serious matters such as remembering (and mostly forgetting) to take the chicken out of the freezer, and wondering whether or not Yu-Gi would win this particular duel tournament or not. As such, I disliked speaking for too long on the phone to relatives in Nigeria, which, among other things, would always cut into the time I had to watch my favourite TV shows. The only exception I would make was when it came to speaking to my maternal grandfather.

My grandfather was a funny man. He would keep hold of newspapers in which important political events were recorded from years before. I was never quite sure what was so significant about these articles that they warranted being stored for so many years after they were written, but I suspected that if my grandpa felt they were worth keeping, then perhaps there were things that could still be gleaned from between those now yellowed pages. Abrupt and straight talking, he was a real 'Say what you mean to say, and don't waste any more words than you need' kind of man. You can see how young ears like mine, which were quick to swivel away from long-winded phone calls, would like him. Over the course of my life he would always check in to ask about my education, my thoughts on current events and my future goals.

I remember one day when I was 7 years old, I swallowed an apple pip on parent's evening and started to panic that it would grow into a tree inside me. My mum was on the phone to my grandpa. She was complaining to him that my primary school teacher had said I was too talkative, too loud, too disruptive in class for the other kids. Passing the phone to 7-year-old me, my mum said, quite stern-faced, 'Your grandfather would like to speak to you.' My slightly shaking hand tensed around the phone as I waited for the lecture I expected to come. However, on that day, my grandpa asked me a simple question that would become a seed that took root in all aspects of my life; it was the reason why striving to be the best that I could be became so normalised for me, and the reason why I learnt from an early age to be confident when establishing a vision for myself, regardless of what others could or could not see. The question was, 'Omo mi, se o fe lo si Oxford abi Cambridge?' meaning, 'My child, do you want to go to Oxford or Cambridge?'

Fast forward several years – after jumping over a few hurdles and catching some unexpected curveballs from life, struggling with depression and anxiety, and subsequently having to take a year out from my studies – and, I (finally) graduated from the University of Oxford, with a degree in English Language and Literature. This time, my grandfather (in a recent conversation, before my first visit to his hometown in Owo, Nigeria) asked me, 'So, Princess, what do you want to do next?' I found myself tongue-tied, muttering something about needing a break and then unconvincingly following up with, 'I might study for my

Masters later.' It is this unanswered question that would keep running circles in my mind during that trip.

The end of one thing,
is the beginning of another.
A road does not end,
so much as change course.

Our car headed out of Murtala Muhammad Airport and we slowly joined the mass of vehicles weaving themselves along the road. Lagos traffic is its own entity for sure. You must factor it into your journey, it is the extra passenger that slips on to the yellow faragon, unnoticed by the beady-eyed bus conductor clinging from the side; you must join the twisting dance of the road with a confident care. Like the mother whose child you watch clinging to her back on the roadside, the slowness of the road grows on you, grows with you, till your eyelids become heavy with fatigue. Hawkers often chance the temper of this slow winding beast. I guess a rumbling stomach, much like an empty fuel tank, must be fed when it cries out in hunger. And everyone is hungry, enterprising. In Nigeria, there are 500 plus languages and dialects, meaning that there are 500 plus ways to make money, all clamouring to be heard above the horns and dust of this busy city. There's always the promise that something entertaining is just about to happen. Lagos is a city that has problems, yet it doesn't give you the time to dwell on them, you either keep moving and find a solution or get left behind with what has now become your very own personal problem. Lagos roads demand that people drop their hopes and dreams of a better Nigeria into their many potholes. It is those dreams that fill in the gaps, and keep them moving over the rough roads like water – knowing despite the obstacles they may face, their journey will not end so much as it will change course. It is a lesson in perseverance that I am reminded of each time I come back home.

PRINCESS PEACE

As we sat in Lagos traffic eating yam and egg in a cab, Mr T, our driver (not that Mr T, I assure you) would quickly insert a white piece of yam into his mouth after each furtive glance at the brief openings made by fellow drivers. I noticed a hawker, weaving and dodging around our car, and asked Mr T what the little bundles of bendy, reedlike canes he was holding were for. He responded that these canes were often used by soldiers at the roadside to show people that they wielded authority and power, how now and again they might be used by an outstretched arm to smack those they deemed to be a nuisance, through the driver's side window. Mr T leaned forward to show me the one he keeps stored by the windshield in front of him, in full view for everyone to see, to signal that they should not mess with the owner of this car. That he is a military man. When I asked him if he had ever been in the army, he responded with a hearty laugh, 'Of course not! But it is dat confidence wey you go carry yourself with, dat go make people treat you de same way.' I turned my head and shared a smile with my reflection in the passenger side window; even in traffic, Lagos is a power-play of a playground. The vibrant essence of fake-it-till-you-make-it. You decide who you are, and you let nobody tell you any different.

On the car radio, a conversation between two Nigerian radio hosts, one who had a London accent and the other a rich Igbo accent, caught my attention. They were discussing the ongoing xenophobic attacks on Nigerians in South Africa, how a lack of jobs and, as a consequence, money, often makes people look for scapegoats. The Igbo man pointed to the Biafran war as his example – the host with a London accent pointed to the Brexit rhetoric around immigration and Donald Trump's 'Build a wall' slogan, as his.

At home, I pick and peel apart the flesh
of an orange in my hand,
watch its citrus spray float across the transatlantic where

a different type of orange sits in a house of white in
    Washington,
where its policies peel apart
the entwined fingers of mothers
from their children.

On arriving at Owo, I stood across the road from the little square
hut that was the first home of my maternal grandparents and
their children, and I learnt from my grandfather's cousin a short
history of their origins. How, after studying in Nigeria they had
briefly come to the UK in the 60s as immigrants, before returning
to Owo and later moving to Lagos. By then, they had already had
four of their eight children, and so I reason that they probably
thought Nigeria would be an easier place to raise them. Unfortunately, I'll never quite know for definite what it was that their
motives were. I know my grandmother was training to be an
architectural assistant (a role scarcely occupied by women at the
time) and my grandfather was a young VIO (Vehicle Inspection
Officer) rising up the ranks in Nigeria. A cousin of my grandpa
told me how he had loved my grandma for her business savvy and
intelligence, how gender had made no difference to him when it
came to studying. Education was the most important thing, an
equaliser of humankind in his eyes – a lesson he instilled in his
grandchildren and a few of the parents in Nigeria whose children
he had helped send to school. I guess being a Yoruba Muslim man
married to a Yoruba Christian woman for over 60 years, defy-
ing the cultural norms of their times was something they were
both accustomed to. After speaking to my grandfather's cousin,
I realised just how much of my grandmother's life was unknown
to me. I wondered why it was that I had never really understood
all that she had accomplished in her career. It's been almost four
years since her passing now, and I wish I could have discussed
her achievements with her whilst she was alive: to know what
her worries and her fears were – how it had felt the first time she

came to London with my grandpa, what it was like to have to put aside her career in order to raise eight children, perhaps, how she thought I might answer my grandfather's haunting question, 'What do you want to do next?'

With my stay in my grandparents' hometown coming to an end, I decided to visit the acclaimed Nike Art Gallery on Lekki Island before heading back to London. It was my first time going to The Islands, where traffic light signals were actually obeyed and smooth concrete roads boasted of government funds not pocketed – the home of the rich elite and anyone else who could afford to dwell there. My first thought was that it reminded me of an experience I'd had whilst growing up as a teen in Hackney. I was around thirteen years of age when I first realised that I had never before had a real reason to journey into the City. I remember being on the 277 bus, headed to a debate competition being held in the City, when it dawned on me. I had only ever seen these glass skyscrapers from afar; this famous London skyline had only ever been a faint backdrop to my world. One only made more tangible whilst sitting near the windows in my French class when I would sometimes turn to gaze like Gatsby at the small light that blinked at the top of Canary Wharf Tower. Leaving mainland Nigeria for the first time to enter into The Islands felt the same. That small, bitter yet wistful, feeling that erupts in the pit of your stomach when you are brazenly faced with such a stark contrast between all that is for a few, and what could be for all. These musings were halted when the owner of the art gallery – whom I had managed to secure an interview with – asked me, 'So my dear, what do you do?' Quick as anything, before I could gather myself to answer her question, my mother intercepted whatever fumbled response I was preparing to give. She answered with a proud, 'This is Princess, my daughter, she just came from Oxford University.' I smiled awkwardly and turned over her phrasing in my mind, how she had made it sound as if I had quite literally come to the gallery straight from the university, how her pride was audible as she concluded, 'She'll be an Oxford graduate at the end of this month.' I smiled outwardly, sighed inwardly and tried not to buckle from the weight of my bittersweet feelings at being introduced in this way.

I doubt my response was completely a symptom of imposter syndrome; I tell myself I've long since sat on the head of that creature, looked it deep in its eyes, and told it I was the captain now (although like most creatures hiding in the deep, it can sometimes resurface unexpectedly). I wouldn't even say that the critical stance I take towards Oxford as a heavily elitist institutional space is solely to blame for the reluctance I feel to claim my mother's title, 'Oxford graduate'. Rather, it's more to do with the feeling that comes after achieving a long-held ambition. The feeling provoked by realising how, when you attain something you have prized for so long – something you and others have made your goal for quite a substantial part of your life – that anchor of purpose that once held you down can quickly become no heavier than a feather. The feeling that your sense of your place in the world is floating away, drifting further each time someone asks you, 'So, what do you do now?' and knowing that more often than not, what they – and what my grandfather – were really asking was, 'So, *who* are you now?'

There is a particular burden one carries in being a daughter to proud, part-immigrant, part-first-generation Nigerian parents and grandparents, whilst negotiating the politics inherent within the hyphenated space that is black-Britishness. Where, on the one hand, you are told to be proud of the tables you are seated at, the ones you worked hard to be seated at; and where, on the other hand, you have learnt from the likes of Audre Lorde, Toni Morrison and Claudia Jones, that it is these same tables that you and your peers should seek to dismantle. You realise how, after you have passed through the British education system wrestling with these contesting positions, the answer to the question 'What's next?' becomes a daunting ideological (and somewhat existential) query. One which the immediate ingrained answer from the Nigerian in me is, 'Whatever I do, I shall be successful,' and yet, where the definition of what that success looks like is ever changing. It's almost easy, then, to allow your response to be shaped for you, for the terms of your existence and achievements to be defined on your behalf.

As a 22-year-old Nigerian black-British woman and a recent graduate, I've come to realise that university truly is just a microcosm of wider society. And that whether you are in higher education or in a working environment, you cannot let worries over what you may or may not face (such as navigating a drunk white student randomly coming up to tell you he would be afraid of you if he were sober, or on entering a communal kitchen area, suddenly becoming the elephant that causes the room to fall silent) to stop you from entering into spaces you wholly deserve to be in. It is even more important then, to allow yourself to express your achievements unafraid. To remember that silence can be weaponised against you. That when you walk into a room and it quietens because you have now disrupted the optics of that space, to remember to speak louder than that which seeks to quieten you. Break it, if for no one else but yourself; break it again, if for no one else but the young black girls who will one day grow up to walk in your wake.

In a world that is often too quick
to teach black women
how to slowly slip silence in-between
the plump space of our lips,
to speak in more hushed tones – we are defiant, bolder and
    unapologetic
with a promise to be greater than our foremothers who
    came before us.

As Loud as Lagos Traffic

As I write this, I'm sitting in a plane heading back to the UK, trying not to despair at trading the cool heat of Lagos during the raining season, for the infamous cold, wet light of British weather. I am a young black woman living in a society where someone like Boris Johnson can spout racist comments about black people being 'piccaninnies' with 'watermelon smiles' and still be voted in as Prime Minister of the British people. Where a black woman MP, Diane Abbott, received almost 50 per cent of the hate-filled tweets sent to female MPs before the 2017 election. I understand all too well how navigating certain institutional spaces and planning out your next steps can seem quite a daunting task.

A proverbial saying that often crops up in my mother's prayers over me comes to mind, 'Olorun maje ki a rin ni ojo t'ebi npa ono,' which roughly translates to, 'God, do not let us walk on the day the road is hungry.' It is not only meant to ward against untimely or unexpected death, but is also a prayer that we will one day reap the benefit of the fruits we sow when we are out on our journeys. She prays it so that I may walk more boldly, make better decisions, be unafraid. After all, it is always harder to see where you are going if your head is constantly held down in fear, or if you wear your achievements like ankle weights in disbelief that you belong on the road you are taking. It's all too easy to forget sometimes that you are allowed to pace yourself. To realise that the drawbacks you may face in life are mere pauses, opportunities to learn how to draw on your power, and not reasons to let your curiosity for life be drawn out of you.

As the wheels of the plane touch down on UK soil once more, that question from the last conversation I had with my grandfather this summer, which, as it turned out, took place just two days before his death (the reason for my visit to his hometown was to take part in the traditional ceremony rites for his burial) crops up once more in my mind: 'So, Princess, what do you want to do next?' I remember how, when I stumbled to quickly find an answer, he chuckled slightly. He reminded me, quietly and in

Yoruba, that no matter what my next steps may be, 'You should be proud of what you've accomplished so far, because your successes aren't just yours alone. They are part of the road laid down by all those who came before you. So you honour them, when you learn to live life as loud as Lagos traffic.' My Oxford graduation ceremony is just two weeks away now, and although I'm still not quite sure what happens next in my life, or in which direction my career path should go, I am no longer afraid of finding out. As my journey back to Nigeria reminded me, I was raised too proud to let my dreams be suffocated by fear.

> Black women:
> we who come from a lineage of pride,
> where being told to work twice as hard was pumped like
>   oxygen through our veins,
> so now the drive to succeed comes as easy as breathing.
> We master life with each breath that we take.

SELINA THOMPSON

Selina is one of our favourite creatives (and frankly, people) in the world and has created some of our favourite things. Yomi first became aware of Selina's intimidating talents in 2015, when she went to see her solo show on Black hair and beauty standards, 'Dark & Lovely', after fangirling over her on Twitter. This was followed by Selina's critically acclaimed 2018 show 'Salt', in which she draws upon her journey retracing the transatlantic slave triangle from Britain to Ghana to Jamaica and back – which Yomi saw twice, and ugly cried at both times. Her ability to tackle often inaccessible and uncomfortable truths with tenderness and humour is why we can't wait for you to read her thirty thoughts on turning thirty.

A Crocus Ruminates:
Thirty Thoughts on Turning Thirty

I'm presuming you're reading this in 2020, which means that, all being well, I'm turning (or turned) thirty this April, to a fanfare of purple crocus buds. I find that when my brain is not full to the brim with work, or mourning the inability of my own knees to keep up with Megan Thee Stallion's,[*] this change is all I think about. It's exhilarating. It feels very new but also laden with possibility. As silly and random as they can be, milestones give us a framework to evaluate the landscape of our lives, and if we so choose, to create change. My thirtieth birthday just so happens to coincide with the change in the decade, so I get to see this play out in the political, as well as the personal.

So, in honour of my thirtieth year, the century's twentieth year, and a decade of watching Black British women continue to slay in the face of spectacular odds, I present my

30 Thoughts on Turning 30

1. Oh God, death is coming.

2. JK!

3. I actually can't wait to turn thirty. The past ten years have been a challenge for me: a challenge that feels bound up,

---

[*] Spell coconut? I can barely spell ouch.

in a way, with the political moments that have occurred over the course of the decade, the economic pressure of being a working class millennial and the additional pressure of living with a bipolar disorder diagnosis (with a side order of epilepsy). Much like my school years, I fetishised my twenties before I entered them, and no reality could have ever lived up to my expectations. For the past twenty years, I realise I have been engaged in a relentless push and pull with my adolescence; and in truth, I am done with it.

4. Thirty feels *very different* from the other milestones I've passed. It is the first milestone birthday that is not defined by a passage from childhood to adulthood, or by being allowed to do stuff. Sixteen was sex and cigarettes, eighteen took the dangerous edge out of clubbing, and twenty-one felt like an extension of eighteen, as though I had been playing at being an adult for three years, and now, suddenly it was real.

5. Thirty, on the other hand, is a whole different beast. Thirty asks you what you have built, and what you wish to keep building or start to build differently. Whether we like it or not, it is a decade full of tensions around fertility and child rearing – for those of us able and inclined towards pregnancy – as hormone levels shift and bodies change; it comes with new-found career pressures and opportunities as we harvest the seeds of our twenties or move on to new soil, and we watch our parents and caregivers enter new phases in their lives, which might change how we relate to them and live with them. We compare ourselves now to where we were at their age, and think about the ways in which the world has changed. We're not the sexy new thing any more, and this is a release of pressure, but perhaps it's a slight shock too.

6. I never did make a thirty under thirty list.

7. I wish we'd get rid of those.

8. It feels like an interesting decade to enter thirty in. Black British women have spent the past ten years getting their elbows, knees and shoulders through a doorway our foremothers pushed their feet through. Whether it's Bernardine Evaristo (the writer of the foreword of this book) winning the Man Booker Prize, or playwright Natasha Gordon's ceiling-breaking West End debut, *Nine Night*; artist Lubaina Himid's Turner Prize, or Baroness Doreen Lawrence's ongoing activism; the historic appointment of activist Lady Phyll as CEO of the charity Kaleidoscope, or the emergence of publications such as *gal-dem*; the staying power of MP Diane Abbott, or Gina Miller being the only person in Britain who seems to understand how our uncodified constitution works, the work has been endless, defined by its tenacity and success. Precedents have been set for me, not only in the past but in the here and now.

9. That being said, the half-in-half-out space of success as a Black woman in a predominantly white country is a complex one. In a recent interview with writer Rianna Jade Parker, photographer Carrie Mae Weems said that, 'Black people are working from the position of "we". We talk about community much more. We talk about who we are as a people emerging out of a situation. We participate differently around the question of social and artistic responsibility and then social possibility.'[1] I often wonder what the responsibility and sense of community that Weems refers to means for Black success. I wonder how, and if, the success of the individual can lead to the institutional

and social change that is needed, and if it cannot, what are the changes that we need to make to our definition of success?

What we perceive to be success so often depends on institutions that are intimately linked to capitalism, white supremacy and the ongoing oppression of the global south – all of which we, as members of a global diaspora, have a very different relationship with to our white peers. Whenever we make gains in visibility and representation we simultaneously risk losing our integrity and political grit, as we become thriving parts of systems that have betrayed us and our communities since their inception. All of this rubs up against our own desire for financial security, and our personal ambitions and dreams. These questions become more urgent as we move out of our twenties, our experience grows and the scope for our successes becomes bigger.

10. It is not just political complicity that is at play here. We also have to consider the longterm impact of excelling in environments where we are expected to code-switch, to leave half of who we are at home, to compromise on lessons we may have learnt from childhood about what matters and why. Throughout my twenties I have felt a move away from such coping mechanisms as I seek to grow into a whole version of myself. I'm lucky: I work in the arts, run my own performance company and exist on the fringes of traditional theatre. There is space for me to decide to be uncompromising in how I express myself. I wonder how I might share this freedom?

11. This is an anthology for loud Black girls, and I am proud to be one. That being said, I feel like so much of the work that has been done around Black womanhood in the past decade – from the emergence of British punk band Big Joanie,

to the ubiquity of phrases such as Black Girl Magic and
Carefree Black Girl, to podcasts such as Thirst Aid Kit and
the stories being told by Michaela Coel, Issa Rae and Cecile
Emeke – has been about showing us in spaces of complexity
and nuance.

This loud Black girl is yearning for opacity, for a space of
quiet reflection right now.

12. I feel like a crocus before spring, somewhere underground,
trying to germinate.

13. From here, beneath the soil, I find that I want to turn away
from excellence.

14. When I say excellence, I'm referring to *the drive*, the
relentless, unforgiving, all-encompassing, completely
insatiable drive to be the best in all that I do. The constant
competition with other versions of myself. Or perhaps it's
competition with others, with those who should be my
sisters, and I am saying 'with myself' to soften the violence
of this thought. Whatever the case may be, there is always
a competition and winning is the only available option.

15. What might an alternative be? Jay Z starts 'Murder to
Excellence' with the words 'Black excellence, opulence,
decadence'. It is fitting that both he and Kanye West,
in thrall as they both are to a vision of Black capitalism
as liberation, present a binary of death or ostentatious
achievement and wealth. I wonder increasingly, about the
value of pushing for excellence, and what its cost is.

16. I wonder about how the demand for excellence and the
hierarchy it necessitates might invalidate the community
thinking that Carrie Mae Weems alludes to.

17. Many of the jibes against millennials centre on the idea of participation awards, of each of us being 'special', and of entitlement. This does not tally with my experience of being tested at every level of my education, of teenage years and then an academic life shaped by the pursuit of excellence. Straight A*s at GCSE and straight A's at A Level, no first in my degree but at least I left with a prize, a smorgasbord of extra-curricular activities, all achieved while almost always working a thirty-hour-per-week job at the same time.

18. This continued into my twenties, which were defined by professional excellence, by agreeing to never-ending requests to work for free, and with no notion whatsoever of professional boundaries. I had no sense of what might be safe and what might not, of who I might be outside of my working life, and what that person might want.

19. It should be said that I don't regret or mourn this. I honour who I have been for the past thirty years, and I am thankful for my focus, hard work and drive. My job has taken me across six continents, given me creative expression, some political agency and even, at times, fun. My career would not have been possible without my education. Choosing to regret it feels odd and counterintuitive. (Over)work has often been a temporary salve to loneliness and isolation for me. It has felt like the answer to the ambitions and sacrifices of our parents.

    This doesn't mean I want more of the same though.

20. I don't think I'm alone in this: I see it in the words of Roxane Gay's *Hunger*; between the pages of *Slay In Your Lane*; in the earnest and well-meaning respectability politics of Michelle Obama's *Becoming*; in the legacy of underappreciated Black women expected to save the world. I don't think it's

necessarily a bad thing. This force, the drive to excel, creates and transforms – and when we succeed? It tells us that we are special, not just in spite of capitalist standards but also *by* them. It is this drive that gently holds our egos together, and as such it has a purpose: ego keeps us going, keeps us sane when all the odds are stacked against us, and the world refuses to see us. God knows Black women need that.

21. At the same time, and since Beyoncé's *Homecoming*, I've been deeply pondering the pitfalls of this drive. I was taken aback by my emotional reaction to watching the documentary: despite its joy and beauty, by the end of it I was furious.

    Witnessing an artist, who has already earned her place amongst the pantheon of legends, putting herself on a diet that comprised of 'No bread, no carbs, no sugar, no dairy, no meat, no fish, no alcohol' only six months after an experience with toxaemia so dangerous it forced her to take bed rest for a month, felt terrifying.[23]

    Like all things pop culture, this terror had very little to do with Beyoncé and everything to do with me. Most of us do not have millions in the bank, nor the machine of Parkwood Entertainment around us to sustain such drive, but in our own ways we each compete and strive with the same vigour. My body bears – in its epilepsy, in its memories of trauma, in its too-long exposure to stress, overwork and exhaustion – the evidence of where I have pushed myself too hard, all for something that felt bigger than myself. Our intentions can be so pure: for the culture, for our ancestors, for our descendants, for our community. We stand in a lineage of sacrifice, and that comes with a weight. But I'm not sure if that weight is freedom.

22. And isn't freedom what all this is for? What historically *all* Black struggle has been for?

23. What does it look like to be 'excellent' in how we practise freedom? In the strength of our spirits?

24. One of the great joys of social media is that it allows us to notice when several folks are making similar small changes. It lets me see a resurgence of Black women looking at their spiritual and physical growth. It lets me see us weightlifting and meditating, changing career and journalling, travelling and dancing and laughing. I feel like we are a shoal of fish, or a flock of birds, gently making a turn together.

25. Let me be clear: this does not mean an abandonment of radical politics.

    I read Akasha Gloria Hull's *Soul Talk: The New Spirituality of African American Women*, early in 2019. It was a pivotal read for me, and one of the things that stuck out was her description of a three-pronged approach to liberation: political activism, creative expression and spiritual healing, and the need for balance across all three. Too much of the politics and you risk burnout and a life without joy, too little and you are caught in neoliberalism. Without creative expression we cut off what it is to be human, but too much and we risk thinking that empty rhetoric is 'the work'. No one wants to slip into 'hotep' territory, with an excess of spirit work that is not grounded in reality; but without it how do you value yourself outside of your job and the opinions of others?

    It's when these three elements are balanced that we get to both fight for freedoms and to live them, and I think this will be my aim going forward.

26. adrienne maree brown starts her beautiful text, *Pleasure Activism*, with the question: 'Who taught you pleasure?'

I want to adapt this a little here, and ask, as I head into another phase of womanhood: Who has taught me what pleasure might look like?

27. I wasn't around when any of my aunts or my mother turned thirty, but I do remember, very clearly, when my mum turned forty. My dad, a quiet, but intensely romantic Aries, organised a surprise party for her. Me and my sister weren't invited, but we got to accompany him on numerous adventures around Birmingham as he plotted, planned and poured all of his passion for her into a surprise dinner party, with her favourite food and people. We were excited to be a part of the secret, and we did get to see her burst into tears when friends she had not seen in years burst out from behind my godmother's sofas to gently terrify her with their affection.

    But I remember thinking, in my nine-year-old way, 'Wow! This person has a whole life, a whole personality, a whole existence apart from me,' and it was the first time I'd really realised that. Her life was abundant with love, and in that moment, joy.

    I hope I will be able to say the same when I reach forty; that, like my mum, I will have continued to nurture the seeds of my twenties, and planted new ones too.

28. Turning forty was a pivotal time for her. She signed up to return to night school the Monday after her birthday party, buoyed by all that support to train to be a teaching assistant, and then a Special Educational Needs Support Worker. She decided she was going to take her children abroad and started saving tenaciously to make it happen. She healed a rift with her father that had separated the two of them since her wedding day, over two decades earlier. She did her healing work.

29. This is such an important part of the lineage of Black women. We remake ourselves at every turn, we learn new skills, we tool up for the coming storm, to reclaim lost youth and freedoms. In getting to do this at thirty, rather than at forty, I bloom in a warmth that my mother has gifted me.

30. But I'm also looking forward to forty.

    I am all ready with my auntie aesthetic: plant-heavy, and vegan I hope, with a lot of food that I grow myself. Dreadlocks, long down my back; earrings Pat Butcher would envy; all-black outfits with neon Doc Martens and very bright accessories, and a bold lip. A library of books across genres and increasingly eccentric jigsaws; a grumpy cat and a basking tortoise to keep me company. Still wafting the fragrance of moderately priced soaps with me everywhere I go, and still, with an encyclopaedic knowledge of each and every Missy Elliott lyric.

    I still won't be able to dance, but perhaps I'll attempt it more often. I still won't be able to run, but I'll have figured out how I want to commune with nature. Maybe I'll have started to take satisfaction from the way in which I paint, and the hit and miss nature of my singing voice.

    If the bipolar persists (it will), I hope it will not kill me.

    I hope the same of the epilepsy.

    If this knee injury heads the way I think it's headed, I at least hope I will have a very sparkly stick to walk with me.

    If I am still fat, I hope I will be in dimpled love with myself.

    There will still be battles to fight. There will be for all my lifetime. I hope I am better at blending theory with action, and that I can do all of this with grace and respect.

I hope I will be respected and active in the live-art community of which I am part, but also a part of my local community. I'll walk a dog in the mornings and head to the leisure centre for Aquafit with the pensioners in the early afternoon.

I shall be nurturing and mentoring and supportive, active and politicised, but from a foundation of joy.

Supporting the other crocuses as they bloom:

Alice Walker Lavender,

Julie Dash White,

Lemonade Yellow.

References

1 Rianna Jade Parker, 'Black People Work from the Position of "We": An Interview with Carrie Mae Weems', *Frieze*, (25 October 2019) <https://frieze.com/article/black-people-work-position-we-interview-carrie-mae-weems>

2 Nicole Saunders, 'Beyoncé Cut Out Carbs, Sugar, Dairy, Meat, Fish, and Alcohol from Her Pre-Coachella Diet', *Harpers Bazaar*, (18 April 2019) <https://www.harpersbazaar.com/celebrity/latest/a27193860/beyonce-coachella-diet-twitter-reactions/>

3 'Beyoncé in Her Own Words: Her Life, Her Body, Her Heritage', *Vogue*, (6 August 2018) <https://www.vogue.com/article/beyonce-september-issue-2018>

SHEILA ATIM

Sheila is a jack-of-all-trades and the master of a great many. She's a former model, a singer and is best known for her work as an actress. Sheila also plays the piano, violin, bass and drums. And unsurprisingly, she is a wonderful writer, bringing her first written play, *Anguis*, to the Edinburgh Fringe Festival last year. Here, she writes with characteristic brilliance about the link between the larger global and political uncertainty and the experience of uncertainty within black women's lives.

What Happens Next?

Astrophysics fascinates me. I love hearing about the universe and of wild hypotheses completely beyond my comprehension. So, when considering what happens next in this world, my mind conjures images of a cosmic black hole and its event horizon – the point of no return. We are hurtling towards a single point at great speed, paradoxically in slow-motion, as time bends. And once we slip over the edge, are we crushed into nothing? Are we reborn into a new entity? Do we pass through unscathed or split into two parts, as Einstein postulated – the escapee watching on as the other is sucked into oblivion? And what if there are multiverses with completely different rules? Weighing up these endless possibilities, scientists circle back to the same place. Right now, we don't know.

Brexit has been a trying ordeal for everyone. Like a leprotic zombie, ridden with shady promises and endless impasses, it hobbles with perseverance to a destination that no one quite understands. Meanwhile, a Trump-shaped elephant in the corner of the room continues to smash through our fine china as we strive to merely live our lives in peace. The cautionary tales surround us; history is repeating, read the signs, heed the warnings! But as patterns emerge, the question of how far our predictions will truly take us in this somewhat unfamiliar world rings like a tolling bell.

The achievements made by black women in the past must not be overlooked. However, the visibility of black women worldwide is reaching a new moment. The conversation around representation, though challenging and imperfect, continues to be on everyone's lips and black women are increasingly reaching the forefront of their respective fields or carving out new territories entirely. But resistance is bound to arise. Pushes towards progress mean counter-pushes. Making waves means expecting backwash. And that's fine – just don't let them stop us, right? Outlast the opponent, dig deep and keep them on the ropes. Well, in theory, yes. And this is a strategy that black women are – willingly or not – indeed familiar with. The acquired ability to endure for the sake of greater advancement. But can endurance alone suffice at this pivotal time?

In 2016, I performed at the National Theatre, London, in a production of *Les Blancs*, written by Lorraine Hansberry and directed by Yaël Farber. Hansberry died of cancer at 34 before completing her final draft. The resulting piece was a posthumous arrangement by her husband and literary executor Robert Nemiroff. The story follows Tchembe, visiting his native African home for his father's funeral. His trip coincides with rising civil unrest within the colonised country and Tchembe is plunged into an ideological tussle between the better life he has pursued in Europe versus all that he has left behind. Ever since he left, he has been plagued by a vision of a woman – an omnipresent force burning in his mind, a reminder of home. I was 'The Woman'. Our version of the character walked with an unrelenting slowness, dogging Tchembe throughout and at one point climbing onto his back, bearing down upon him the same heavy weight as her steps carried. She summoned something of the ancestral with her clear call to action. But she never spoke.

The sole black female character in a play set in Africa and she does not utter a single word. Was this a problem? Would this nameless and mute depiction serve as an erasure of black women?

Would it oust them from their own stories as is so often the case? Well, Yaël contested that it was a knowing and intentional statement by this successful black female writer. She was commenting on the larger voicelessness experienced by us all and as her cancer advanced, she too grew ever more voiceless in a literal sense. The production was well received and for the overwhelming majority, The Woman's silence spoke volumes. She began the whole production by turning the revolving stage, which continued to spin throughout and she ended by holding two horns aloft and rotating in front of a burning building. There was no negating her indisputable power.

The parallel between The Woman and black women throughout the African diaspora is not a difficult one to draw. She held so much potential that she could not vocalise – a sad and deeply frustrating existence. The Woman's call to Tchembe was not a gentle tap on the shoulder. She was in pain, as were her people, and despite her slow gait, her urgency and desperation were palpable. The time is now. Much like holding one's breath underwater, the pressure is building and the need to inhale mounts. And yet to live constantly underwater and still not drown is to remain trapped in this agonising state. One lives, but with few other options than to maintain course, albeit with a tension in the chest that cannot be relieved. So – the solution is a simple one. We just need the outlet, the mode of expression, the voice. The chance to reach the surface and gulp the air. Surely?

In 2017, I played the title role in *Babette's Feast* written by Karen Blixen (under the pseudonym Isak Dinesen), adapted by Glynn Maxwell and directed by Bill Buckhurst. The story follows a French woman's escape from the nineteenth century Franco-Prussian war to a small religious village in Denmark, where she lives with two sisters. On her arrival, she is simply a refugee who cannot speak the language. Over the years, she remains mysterious but quietly adheres to the sisters' very simple and pious way of life. Babette's true identity, however, is that of a famous chef and her life back in France was much more vivacious. It is only when a ceremonial occasion approaches that Babette offers to cook a feast for the community, using the money she had won from a French lottery ticket she's finally redeemed. This is her only remaining possession and Babette has waited many patient years for the ideal opportunity to use it. The meal preparations are a much more decadent affair than the village is comfortable with but after embracing the proceedings, a good time is had by all.

Babette's story echoes the experiences of many who traverse lands to seek better lives and opportunities. Think of those stuck in the Calais Jungle or the passengers of *SS Windrush*. How are they met in their new surroundings? Can they make peace with what's left behind? What currency do they have in this new place? Those with positions of prestige in their old countries find themselves plunged into worthlessness in the new. Voicelessness. Our Babette was also black, something not originally specified in the play but a nuance that further teased out the undertones of alienation and otherness. Babette carried a culture and history with her that was completely unlike that of the Danish village. She would always feel a subtle rift between herself and the place that she had grown to call home. This predicament is mirrored in the experiences of black British women of all generations, be it immigrant, first or later the ever-raging identity battle triggered by life in the UK, a place currently engaged in its own conflict. Is this truly my home or am I just a lodger here? And should we be inside the EU or out?

Babette fulfilled her wish. She offered the village something they had never experienced and brought herself a little closer to her former life by practising her art. But with all the money from the ticket gone, this was only ever to be a one-night affair, a fate she accepted before she began. Additionally, her guests, whilst grateful, would never truly appreciate the depths of what she had gifted them that night. 'It is unbearable to be an artist; to be applauded for doing your second best' – her last words reverberate as a haunting reminder that the vastness of her wish will never truly be fulfilled. She gets the voice that The Woman never had. But there are caveats. Her expression is limited. It cannot and never will be her voice in its entirety and though the moment itself is wonderful, it is also the source of a deep pain driven by unsated desire. She reached the water's surface and gulped one mouthful of air. It was not enough. A space for black women within British and Western cultures has been carved out through rigorous effort and determination. But is this space sufficient? How often has this 'seat' felt more akin to a backless stool? The opportunities exist but they are clipped, limited, monitored so as not to exceed the quota. Meanwhile, these same cultures are awash with inspiration acquired from black women but with no due credit awarded. From music to fashion to language and vernacular. Celebrities flaunt their 'boxer braid' cornrows. Lip fillers and buttock implants create a fuller look that black women have been historically maligned for. A famous young country singer took the 'twerk' to new heights. Our offerings do not appear to be valuable until they have been proffered by a more palatable set of hands.

So, the opportunity to merely speak in a world such as ours is not enough on its own. If The Woman could talk, she would likely be in a noisy room with a timekeeper's thumb hovering eagerly over a stopwatch – you have fifteen minutes to express a lifetime. Maybe the solution is to shout louder? Overrun the time limit? Fly in the face of those who try to contain us? Surely? Yes, we *could* do that, although once again the path is not straightforward. But even so, credit must be given to the notable black women who have paved paths by taking this approach. Women like Emilia.

In 2018, I played Emilia at the Globe Theatre in a production of Shakespeare's *Othello*. Emilia is an unwitting accomplice to her husband Iago's nefarious plot to destroy Othello. Her desire to win his favour and save their ailing marriage conflicts with her honest nature and she tells a white lie by giving him Desdemona's handkerchief – an act she believes will be largely harmless. Once the fatal consequences of the deceit are revealed, Emilia bares all in an explosive exposé of Iago's lies and malicious intentions.

My take on Emilia was that of a loving, exuberant black woman with an assertive streak. She was more Desdemona's friend than lady-in-waiting and she spoke relatively freely about sex and the women's plight. However, her final act of insolence results in her death. Emilia ceases to play her role as a cog in Iago's evil plan by boldly decrying his crimes. He murders her as a result.

Whilst not *every* act of loud defiance from a black woman results in literal death, once again the parallels here are evident. Our Emilia was confident and quick-witted and despite the private strain in their marriage, Iago still refrained from openly chastising her with too heavy a hand. But this was conditional, with the proviso that she serve his ulterior motives, whether knowingly or not. Freedom was granted but within boundaries. Her tell-all performance did not fall within these boundaries. In the script, not only does Iago kill Emilia, but he slaughters her *after* the truth is already out, rather than in a desperate attempt to silence the singing canary. Surely he is bound to die in any case. There is nothing to be gained from her death at that point. So, it seems his act moves beyond self-preservation and serves instead as a punishment. She betrayed him. She stepped out of line. And despite his inescapable fate, he will not go down unless her life is also ended.

The violence of this act illustrates the aggressive fervour with which marginalised groups are silenced by their opposition when they are asserting themselves or, even worse, thriving. This desire goes beyond merely serving their own selfish interests and finds emotional satisfaction from the act of oppression itself. It provides a salve, a soothing remedy to their frustrations. And this resistance is not only impassioned but irrational, an emotion that eludes the grip of Reason and Common Sense. A dangerous prospect. If driven by senselessness, there is no telling how far one would go to silence the other. So, how safe is it to go audaciously against the grain? To do a 'Simone Biles' and endure threats of disqualification for her brazen gymnastic brilliance? The fight to stay afloat at the sea surface, guzzling all the air one can muster, is to risk being even more aggressively pulled down to the ocean depths. And who knows when you will resurface.

Emilia is probably based on Emilia Bassano, a contemporary and collaborator of Shakespeare's, often named 'The Dark Lady' in his writings. She too was daring, founding a women's writing group in the seventeenth century. Though her definitive race is disputed, a dark-skinned, likely mixed-heritage woman living in Britain was left largely absent from history's mainstream recognition and swallowed by Shakespeare's dominance in the canon of British literature. In 2018, Morgan Lloyd Malcolm debuted her play *Emilia* on the same stage as my *Othello* to help resurrect her voice 400 years after it had been drowned.

In presenting these ideas, I must be clear I do not suggest that black British women should cower or moderate themselves. That can never be a solution. But the uncertainty of this time prompts me to make these interrogations. I am a ruminator and an only child. I need space and solitude to process and ponder. My now-deleted Twitter feed was at odds with that dynamic. However, it was intriguing to observe a singular platform where almost everything in the world's consciousness today is constantly colliding. Feminism, racism, LGBTQ+ rights, Brexit, Trump, natural disasters, SpongeBob memes, fashion, music, theatre reviews, celebrities, comedians, what happened today, what happened yesterday, what might happen tomorrow on both a personal and global scale. In particular, watching the development of Brexit, the far right and black female empowerment in concurrent real-time has been illuminating. Black women are celebrating of themselves and each other directly, cutting out the middle man and coming together to find their own self-generated support system. The far right do the same. Black women are passionately calling out the injustices they believe have been committed against them and their community. Leave and Remain voters do the same. In one snapshot of my phone screen, I would see glowing tweets of empowerment followed by anger-fuelled rants. Trolls and nay-sayers commenting on posts of solidarity and love. An article on the post-referendum spike in hate crimes, right after a celebratory #blackgirlmagic post. All on the same feed. I empathise with an exhausted nation discontented with our politicians for the state of Brexit negotiations. And yet I learned that half of all hate tweets directed at female politicians in the run-up to the June 2017 elections were levelled at one person alone – Diane Abbott.

These issues all appear to be weaving sometimes crashing head on in their discourse and sometimes snaking past each other in their own blissful ignorance. A mixture of cavernous echo chambers and explosive pressure pots. How does one gauge anything about anything anymore? There are too many inter-actions to count. Too many trajectories and factions. How do we garner a clear understanding of what we are all really up against and how do we press forward? The black woman's voice requires a great deal more negotiation when endeavouring to push to the forefront. Sad but true. And now that we've found a rhythm, how do we find longevity and sustainability? Political flux is disrup-tive and the risk of derailment is too great in a time when we are reaching down to anchor some roots.

In 2019, I wrote a play called *Anguis*, which debuted at the Edinburgh Fringe Festival. A modern-day doctor, Kate Williams, meets Queen Cleopatra in a podcast interview that doesn't quite go as planned. As we learn more about both women, we see Kate grappling with the several duties she feels have been placed upon her. Though race is not central to the play, as ever, her blackness has an impact on her experiences, thoughts and actions. The play is a conversation that I often have in my own head, spewed out onto a page. What is my role here? How best do I proceed to serve both myself and my people? Who even *are* my people? In times of uncertainty such as the one we find ourselves hurtling towards, this questioning dials up its frequency and I feel its anxiety pulsing through our collective subconscious. Where do I stand in the various fights I will face and how do I keep on track? I cannot say I have an answer at this time but I do believe that sheer endurance alone, a tactic at which black women have become largely adept, requires updating. By combining the elements of the three fictional characters detailed above – persistence, precise opportunism and a front-kick through the door – there must be a way to elevate us to something even more potent. Imagine once again The Woman with a voice, only this time Babette steals the timekeeper's watch and Emilia hushes the crowd with a captivating warm-up act. She is no longer bound to her fifteen minutes. She is amplified through the diverse collective. Black women in the UK must employ all that has been learned throughout history to build unshakeable foundations and lean on each other's shoulders whilst we lift the bricks in place. In doing so, new paths will present themselves. Surely? Surely.

I have just finished shooting the film *Bruised*, starring and directed by American actress Halle Berry. To date, she is still the only black woman to win an Academy Award for Best Actress in a Leading Role and this film is her directorial debut. Watching her at work as an actor-director has been an unforgettable experience and one that has galvanised me to push my own personal endeavours even further than before. So, as the anxious chatter of 'what comes next?' buzzes restlessly in my thoughts, I am heartened to know that even as the event horizon approaches, with ambitious determination, we continue.

SIANA BANGURA

Siana Bangura is a writer, producer, performer and community organiser hailing from South East London. Across her portfolio of work, Siana's mission is to help move marginalised voices from the margins, to the centre. Reading Siana's writing you can't help but feel moved. It makes you sit up and want to take in every word she has to say. Here, she sets out an inspirational – and provocative – 'Black Feminist 10-point Programme for Transformation'. She challenges the idea of 'a seat at the table' and, in these uncertain times, she emphasises the necessity of creating viable options for alternative futures. As she says, 'the time for squeezing into inadequate spaces is well and truly over'.

'Who built it and with what wood?': A Black Feminist 10-point (ish) Programme for Transformation

For a long time, Black women have been asking for seats at tables created by toxic people upholding a toxic status quo. When they didn't give us a seat – in the words of Shirley Chisholm – we started 'bring[ing] a folding chair'. But I'm sick of this table we keep speaking of, because I don't think anybody is asking questions about the table itself. It's not enough to 'be invited' to have a seat at someone else's table. Why aren't we deeply interrogating who built the bloody table and with what wood?

My friend Jamelia – Birmingham born and raised singer, TV presenter, and all-round babe and national treasure – asked these questions and was dissatisfied with the answers so she built her own table for Black women, including me, to sit at in the form of her latest project, 'Jamelia Presents . . . The Table'. The YouTube series shows conversations with Black women and other members of the Black community exploring everything from careers, motherhood, Taking Up Space, Black British History, Black hair, and the British media. In her own words, she was 'done sitting at tables where [she had to] bring [her] own chair, squeeze into inadequate space and prove why [she] should be there'. Indeed, in 2020, as we find ourselves living in a time of crisis, we urgently need solutions and viable options for alternative futures: the time for squeezing into inadequate spaces is well and truly over – there is no room for that in this new decade. As Jamelia sings in the beautiful opening soundtrack to the series: 'Ain't nothing about my silence golden'.

Too often, owing to the need to be reactive and firefight, very few of us have the time to actually stop and think about what we are fighting to create, in place of what currently exists. I've learnt, after many years of building – sometimes at great emotional cost to myself – that the work of pausing to imagine is a vital step in the process of taking meaningful action.

I have been thinking of the type of world I'd like to live in, what it looks like, and what it would take to build it. In the words of Angela Davis, I've been motivated by the fact 'I [can] no longer [accept] the things I cannot change and so I am [trying to change] the things I cannot accept.'

It is in this spirit – inspired by the Black Panther Party's Ten-Point Program and Rojava's Charter of the Social Contract (look it up if you've never heard of it) – that I offer you a Black feminist 10-point (ish) programme for transformation as a starting point for our collective re-imagining of our existence.

1. Take Up Space and Use Your Voice

Many people are talking about taking up space. I've spoken about it a lot, especially in the years between 2013 and 2016.

2013 was arguably a turning point in our political and social landscape. Margaret Thatcher passed away, as well as Hugo Chavez and Nelson Mandela. Words like 'twerk' and 'selfie' were added to the English dictionary and the issue of gay marriage divided America. Most significantly, the trial of George Zimmerman – the vigilante who murdered African-American teenager Trayvon Martin in cold blood – took place, with a 'not guilty' verdict on all counts delivered on 13 July of that year. That same day, Zimmerman's acquittal resulted in the #BlackLivesMatter hashtag emerging on social media and the online campaign quickly followed.

As the world continued to shake, we bore witness to countless cruelties and injustices, meted out with no apparent consequences. As the power of social media was being brought to the fore, a generation of millennials were coming of age among the noise. This generation – my generation – are the collateral damage. We are the generation of daunting (and rising) student debt; falling or stagnating incomes; the ongoing consequences of the 2008 financial crash and continuing financial insecurity; rising costs of living, including skyrocketing rent and house prices; under-employment, zero-hour contracts and unemployment; privatisation; austerity; Brexit; a resurgence of white nationalism, raging anti-Blackness and of course the reign of Trump and Boris Johnson.

With the odds stacked firmly against us in the tangible, offline world, it was to the nebulous digital and online space that many of us first turned in those years, in order to gain some form of control and find a sense of 'community'. That's where we first found our voices. Twitter, in particular, although founded in 2006, gained significant traction in the years 2011–2013, becoming a key platform for the emergence of 'woke', 'conscious' and politically active young voices, most notably 'Black Twitter'.

Having started as an online community, Black Twitter moved offline. In my case, my platform 'No Fly on the WALL' brought people together IRL – we started taking up space physically in 2014 at Common House, in Bethnal Green. I founded No Fly on the WALL in 2013, to create a platform that would centre the voices and experiences of Black British women and Black women living in the UK, in direct response to my feelings of simultaneous hypervisibility and invisibility, as well as the isolation

I experienced straight after graduating from the University of Cambridge. Little did I know at that time how significant this grassroots, experimental and radically organised space would become in my life for the next four years.

No Fly on the WALL's monthly sista circles, events, workshops and other activities were grounded in our four key pillars: Taking Up Space; (Un)Learning; Creating Safe Spaces; and Community Empowerment. In establishing ourselves as a safe(r) space for Black women's voices, in all their broadness and diversity – and on occasion, other marginalised voices from the different communities to which we belong – No Fly on the WALL followed directly in the footsteps of work done by our foremothers in Britain, as part of a rich history of Black women organising and resisting in the UK. In 1978, Stella Dadzie and Olive Morris founded the Organisation of Women of African and Asian Descent (OWAAD), placing the unique experiences of women of Black and Asian descent firmly on the Women's Liberation agenda. OWAAD itself was a product of work done by preceding groups such as the African Students' Union and politically Black organisation, Southall Black Sisters.

Over the last few years, the shape of how Black women in particular are taking up space and using their voices has changed. There are more online platforms and offline organisations centring the voices and experiences of Black women; there are more individual Black women who have gained success in the mainstream, publishing books, starring in films, building large audiences in a world of 'influencers', leading initiatives, soaring in their professions and in academia, and there are more spaces available for us to speak our truth. However, alongside this, the trend for corporations – and people within our own communities – to exploit our struggle for their self-interest has also intensified (see point 4 on Capitalism). Individual instances of success in a rigged system are not a sign of our collective liberation. But Black women in particular speaking up – often at great cost to ourselves – has been a catalyst for change. We must continue to use our voices, be visible and take up space – and other voices need to be speaking truth to power along with us, criticising the status quo, and sharing the burden. In the words of Rihanna, 'tell your friends to pull up'.

2. Language Matters: No More BAME – We are GMPs (Global Majority Peoples)

Are you tired of people using Woman of Colour (WoC), Person of Colour (PoC) or Black and Minority Ethnic (BAME) when they really just mean Black? Yeah. I'm tired of that shit too. Although at times it is useful to speak of groups, more often than not this homogenisation serves to erase the Black from BAME. Even worse, we're so used to speaking in euphemisms, folks are even using the phrase 'diverse colleagues' when they mean colleagues who are not white. Who and what are we divergent from? What is the standard and why? Why define us by what we are not instead of what and who we are? It's time to throw all of that in the bin. Language matters deeply and we must move away from being afraid to call things – and people – what and who they are. It is not racist to speak of Black people. It is racist to deny that you see colour. It is racist for difference to be a problem. And speaking in these euphemisms allows whiteness to hide in plain sight (see point 3), which we have seen is dangerous.

Although the initial buzz of the movement may have died down, Black lives *still* matter and we mean BLACK lives. According to 2011 Census Data the Black/African/Caribbean/Black British population was approximately 3.3 per cent and yet we are disproportionately represented in poverty statistics, poor housing and homelessness. We are over-represented in the prison system but our plight is grossly under-reported: there are more Black people jailed in England and Wales proportionally than in the USA.*

And let's not ignore the pandemic-sized elephant in the room. The Covid-19 outbreak has not been the 'great leveller' some have claimed it to be but instead, it has exacerbated existing social inequalities. Although the true impact of the outbreak – along with an accurate death toll – may never be known, we do know that once again, Black people in the UK have bore the brunt of this disaster. The Office for National Statistics found that Black women (defined as Black Caribbean, Black African and Black other) are 4.3 times more likely to die from Covid-19 than white women, while Black men were 4.2 times more likely to die. The report went on to say that these alarming disparities seem to be 'partly a result of socio-economic disadvantage and other circumstances, but a remaining part of the difference has not yet been explained'. It's no mystery – structural inequality kills.

Even after taking into account age, demographic factors and measures of self-reported health problems, people in the Black community were still almost twice as likely to die from Covid-19 than white people in the UK (and we haven't even spoken about the fact that in the USA, Black Americans represent 13.4% of the American population, but counties with higher black populations account for more than half of all Covid-19 cases and almost 60% of overall deaths according to reports from CNN).

In addition to the real life consequences of injustice and not giving it its proper name, persisting in referring to Black and Brown people – members of the world's global majority – as 'minorities', enforces a 'minority complex' and reinforces the claim that whiteness is superior. (Let's face it – it isn't but we have been tricked over the last five hundred years to believe it is.)

---

* In the USA the proportion of Black people incarcerated is four times greater than their population percentage; in the UK, this proportion is seven times greater. (See point 8.)

So instead, for the times when it is necessary to group us all together, I argue that we should move away from terms like PoC and BAME (primarily used in the UK) and move towards a term like Global Majority Peoples (GMP). It's not perfect, but I think it's more fit for purpose. Language changes and evolves, as we know, so the more of us who start using this, and the more often, the closer we will get to it being solidified in our everyday parlance, replacing acronyms like BAME. Will there be resistance? Sure. The moment you no longer speak of yourself as a minority or someone powerless, is the moment your oppressor realises you are conscious of your oppression.

3. White Supremacy Must Fall (and White Fragility Along With It)

Everything is about race. Therefore ending white supremacy has to happen, or all of our efforts to build alternative futures will be futile. At this point, I don't think I need to write extensively about why white supremacy continues to screw over everyone who is not white. But I would like to emphasise that it's not down to Black women to end white supremacy. As part of a lethal cocktail of patriarchy, heteronormativity and of course capitalism, there can be no justice while whiteness continues to terrorise the world. Its greatest trick? Convincing white people that it doesn't even exist.

Calling whiteness by its name, leaning into the discomfort, and white people moving away from defensiveness and white fragility are all a good start. The next steps are then to make some personal sacrifices: these include calling out the bullshit of other white people, being willing to lose friends, family, acquaintances and opportunities in the same way that Black, Brown and other GMP folk (see point 2) have had to, and paying reparations (this isn't just about money, it's about time and resources too – see the work of Esther Standford-Xhosei on reparations and reparative justice). Interestingly, a *YouGov* study conducted in 2014 showed that only 6 per cent of white Americans support cash payments to the descendants of slaves, compared to 99 per cent of Black Americans. Similarly, only 19 per cent of whites – and 63 per cent of Black people – support special education and job training programmes for the descendants of slaves. No doubt if a similar study was done in the UK the results would be similar. Talk is cheap – meaningful action from white people is what we need.

4. Understand that Capitalism is Killing Us

Contrary to what Margaret Thatcher proclaimed, there *are* alternatives to capitalism. But nobody gives up their power without a fight. Although the origins of capitalism are complicated, they roughly stretch back to the sixteenth century. When the British systems of power largely collapsed after the Black Death, a newly formed class of merchants began to trade with foreign countries and this newfound demand for exports started to dictate overall production and pricing of goods. Workers were forced to sell their labour in a hierarchical system built on the backs of the poor. And guess what? It also led to the spread of colonialism, slavery and imperialism. By the eighteenth century, England had transformed into an industrial nation.

The impact that capitalism has on your life depends on whether you're a worker selling your labour or a boss holding the means of production. Supply and demand is a key principle, as is consumption and greed. Greed supposedly drives profits and profits drive innovation and product development, which means there are more choices available for those who can afford them. The Occupy Movement, beginning in 2011, and inspired by the Arab Spring of 2010–2012, highlighted the fact that 'the 1 per cent' – the richest of the rich of the capitalist class – were allowed to grow fat wallets unchecked and unchallenged whilst the 99 per cent remained exploited.

Interestingly, studies have been done on the changing attitudes of millennials and it seems many are highly critical of capitalism and are interested in exploring alternatives to it. And it's important to emphasise that Black Capitalism is not what we need either – in the same way I don't want to swap the white man's knife in my back for that of a white woman's, I also don't want the white foot on my neck to be replaced by a Black one.

5. Decolonise 'Diversity'

So many radical ideas and useful terms become watered-down and rendered meaningless by their mainstreaming. An example of this is the word 'intersectionality' – a useful term coined by Kimberlé Crenshaw to describe the ways our different identities are interlinked in their oppression – it has been ruined by white vegans using it to compare animal oppression to racism, slavery and the African genocide. (No matter how strongly you feel about the rights of animals, it is wrong to co-opt other people's slavery to make your point.) 'Diversity' is also now a wishy-washy corporate term, meaning nothing at all. The same goes for 'inclusivity' and worryingly it feels like 'decolonise' may be the next victim.

A public service announcement to everyone: stop wasting our time. No more 'diversity' or 'inclusion' – it is time for decolonising and radical transformation. This means dismantling all systems of oppression. This means decolonising our minds, hearts, language, behaviours, curriculum, histories, philosophies, media – everything. In the words of Lavinya Stennett, 'The process [of decolonising] therefore requires individuals to leave behind the arrogance that accompanies power and apathy that prohibits the space to examine an iniquitous condition objectively . . . In order to decolonise, we have to recognise each facet of life as constituting a work which extends, but is not limited to, the realms of knowledge, territorial/physical space and the body.'

6. Understand that Black History is Global History

And start treating it as such. It should not be squeezed into just one token month of the year. Although we may need Black History Month right now, I hope we won't always need it, because Black History will be embedded in the very fabric of curricula in our primary and secondary schools, as well as universities and workplaces. This is vital for Black people, but also other people – *especially* white people. Ignorance of one's history damages the oppressor as well as the oppressed.

7. Understand that Access to Tools for Mental Wellbeing are a Right not Luxury

What are the things that contribute to poor mental health? Poor housing, racism, police brutality, racialised policing, poor access to healthcare and poor treatment in healthcare settings, inequality, lack of opportunities – diminished mental wellbeing is a reasonable response to this kind of oppression. Access to the tools we need to thrive, not just survive, are not a luxury but a right. Self-care has been commercialised but in its most radical form, in the words of Audre Lorde, 'Caring for myself is not self-indulgence, it is self-preservation, and that is an act of political warfare.'

And whilst we're on the subject of what causes mental illness and mental health issues . . .

8. Let's Abolish the Police (and Address Britain's Prison Industrial Complex)

I know – you're not ready for this conversation yet. But at some point you will need to be. We need to create new forms of transformative collective justice. The police in their current form are mired in colonialism and were set up to protect 'property' and quell political dissent. I know you're thinking 'so what do we replace them with?' The answer to this has to be a collective one.

When it comes to the ways that the policing and carceral systems fail the Black community, and Black women specifically, finding statistics is challenging. Black women are over-represented in prison, making up 26.4 per cent of the female prisoner population. It's no coincidence that the very first person to be arrested under the new Corona Virus Bill was a Black woman, in what was described as 'shambolic' circumstances. Yet despite Black womanhood being criminalised at a disproportionate rate in Britain, very few studies, reports, or meaningful statistics are readily available. Google 'Black British women in prisons' and the first images to come up include Piper Chapman and Alex Vause from *Orange is the New Black:* two white American women.

The harrowing story of Sarah Reed, a Black British woman who died in custody in 2016 in Holloway Prison, brought to light the insidious nature of recurring institutional racism in Britain and the particular toll of state failures on the lives of Black women in Britain. Although there is still scant work on this subject, the mistreatment of Black women by the state and in particular the police is something we should all be alarmed about. This is one of the reasons I produced a documentary, called *1500 & Counting*, on the subject of policing in the UK, following the deaths of Sheku Bayoh and Sarah Reed. Look up the United Families and Friends Campaign, Inquest, and the Institute of Race Relations for more on this subject and then support their work with your coin and your time. The bottom line is we have seen that if the state wishes to undo its punitive measures – such as ensuring early release for low-risk prisoners in response to a global crisis – it can choose to do so, and do so pretty swiftly.

9. Understand that a Black Feminist Analysis is Needed in the Conversation about Climate Justice

It's time to stop talking about the 'threat of climate change' and acknowledge that it is here; it has arrived; it is happening right now. Parts of the world are on fire – literally. No more shortcuts and lazy analysis.

But also, no more white faces at the front on this matter.

The dearth of Black voices, particularly Black female voices, in modern environmentalism means there is a lack of critical analysis from an intersectional Black feminist standpoint on how climate change will uniquely affect Black women and women of colour.

This is not to say that Black women aren't doing the work to tackle climate change – we are – but our work is being invisibilised, as always. Women make up the majority of the world's most economically disadvantaged people and therefore are often the main victims of natural (as well as man-made) disasters. For example, women accounted for 61 per cent of fatalities caused by Cyclone Nargis in Myanmar in 2008; 70–80 per cent in the 2004 Indian Ocean tsunami; and 91 per cent in the 1991 cyclone in Bangladesh. Even when women survive the calamitous event itself, the aftermath is just as perilous. When Hurricane Katrina hit New Orleans in 2005, 80 per cent of those left behind in the Lower Ninth Ward after the storm were women. Ten years after Hurricane Katrina displaced 40,000 people in New Orleans, opinions about the recovery can be traced along racial lines, with new studies underscoring that African American women, particularly those who lived in public housing, faced some of the biggest hurdles after the storm. These facts cannot be ignored. The climate conversation and ensuing actions to save our planet need to centre the voices of GMP folk, the Global South, Indigenous peoples, and Black feminist voices.

If they do not, we are simply replicating the white supremacy, colonialism and exploitation that got us into this mess in the first place.

10. Freedom and Dignity for All Black People – Not Just Some

We cannot pick and choose which of us gets to be free – that is exceptionalism. Freedom must include the poor, working classes, the ill, the disabled, differently abled, trans, non-binary, LGBTQIA+, queer, fat, thin, ratchet, aliens, those in the West, the Global South, educated, not educated, differently educated, among us.

Too often when we say, 'Black lives matter' (see point 2) we mean 'Black cisgender heterosexual men's lives matter (only)', meaning any Black life that deviates from this will not be mourned, acknowledged, or fought for. It is within this context that Black women have been rising up, and it's why we have come to learn that if we do not fight for ourselves, nobody else will. It is no coincidence that the Black Lives Matter movement was co-founded by three Black women (Patrisse Khan-Cullors, Opal Tometi and Alicia Garza). It is also no coincidence that the platforms, movements and projects created by Black women have used a more group-centred model of leadership, rather than the traditional (and hypermasculine) charismatic leadership model of earlier eras.

In the words of Martin Luther King in his letter from Birmingham Jail: 'Injustice anywhere is a threat to justice everywhere.'

Nobody should be left behind.

And I know I've called this a ten-point programme but I'm throwing in a bonus one because I can:

11. Black Joy Must Be at the Forefront of it All

Let's face it: this struggle is a lifelong one – and that is not a loss. What is a loss, is if we can never find time for joy along the way. I've had enough of the consumption of Black grief, pain, sorrow and strife. Striving for Black joy must be central in our quest. It is foundational for any vision of freedom.

As much as there is suffering, cruelty and calamity everywhere, there is also resistance, there is also love, and there is always us.

SOPHIA THAKUR

If you haven't read Sophia's poetry before then you are in for a treat. She's an award-winning poet who is known for pushing traditional boundaries of poetry and literature to inspire audiences across the country and has performed her work at some of the UK's biggest music festivals and venues (Glastonbury, Lovebox, Roundhouse, Tate Britain and many more). Liz was moved by her work when she first saw Sophia perform at Stylist Remarkable Women Awards in 2019 and knew she had to contribute to this anthology. In this essay, addressed to her daughter she writes elegantly and movingly about belonging, motherhood and letting herself – and her child – be loudly themselves. It's a hymn of hope to a change that she feels is in the air and the future she believes is on its way.

A Poem for Babygirl

The much outweighs the few when I think of what I'll tell you.
May my mouth know only to speak of days I wish to be almost as
beautiful as you. And I'm working on making any warnings that
I might have for you become as foreign to me as my own Mother
was to London, Croydon in 1990. Certain seeds plant themselves
into the soil of newly drying skin. Nobody told my Mum and her
sisters about what the English weather could do to a face that
has only ever faced the sun. Through cracking lips and drying
tips, they found the feeling of foreign tucked into every corner
of their day. From being reminded of the things they shouldn't
say, to hiding as much of Africa as they could, away. Except it's
hard to hide a face. Their own Mother may have brushed off as
much of home as she could from their tongues, but accents have
a way of tying you to where you've come from. So even if pid-
geon English was slowly flying from their syntax back into a sky it
wasn't made to shy away from . . . some words just hadn't learnt
the lick of these Gambian women. 'L' still struggled to be heard
in 'palm oil' and only ever seemed to scream in 'Hallelujah'. God
became a necessity to the oldest child trying to be an example
to four younger siblings in a land she herself was still learning.
Mum doesn't really believe me when I tell her how remarkable
she is.

It was survival to her. And I suppose a tiger doesn't expect a
medal for catching the family prey. It was just what it had to do

to get by. Mum had two boys before me, and me at 16 was her first introduction to what happens when London has had years to grow its vines around veins. She clicked straight back into survival mode the day I came home and said I wanted to read in the school poetry competition. I had just learnt about the Biafra War and the Civil Rights Movement and like any newly enraged teenager, begun kindling my disdain towards the empire. I led with a poem. The poem spoke unsubtly on power imbalance, privilege, savagery, cowardice and how racism has injected the structures that govern us today. The poetry competition rules stated that you'd have to read your poem at a Literature Night in front of the governing body, parents and pupils, and the head of GCSE English in England at the time. That was the kind of school I went to. We had a literature night.

Somehow I don't think the organisers had expected it to become a speakers' corner but teenage Sophia was riled up. 'There's no way that you are reading this at the literature night,' was how the conversation with my Mother went. I recognised this as her survival mode. I'm guessing it was a mix of not wanting to impose on anyone's comfort, but also not to encourage such a loud step up into my blackness. Because if I did this, it would be only then that they would know that I was black . . . right?

Mum grew up having to teach her blackness to whisper, and her African-ness to think and feel but never speak. I suppose I can't blame her. Loud blackness came at a painful price when she was a teenager. But I let myself be loud on that microphone nonetheless. I watched as enjoyment was replaced by anxiety on the faces of my parents as I began talking about how far we haven't come as a people, and how black people should be left to sleep for longer because we needed more King dreams to bring about more change. I can't imagine what was going through my Mum's head at this point. Not only had I disobeyed her, but I had done so with her in the audience.

A Poem for Babygirl

Mum and I share the same face. As I read my poem out that evening, I wonder whether she wondered whether people would know that she was my Mother. I know that, now, 10,000 poems and ten years on, she's proud that she gave me her own Father's eyes and Mother's cheekbones. Things are different now. Today I'm paid to offend those who don't see the value in sharing power. (And I won that poetry competition.)

Mum used to sing Ella Fitzgerald's 'Summertime' to me as if it were a nursery rhyme. She wouldn't do this in 2019. Too much has changed. Mummy is rich now and also good looking and that's the standard. Nobody is telling their daughter to 'hush' anymore. At least not directly. Things aren't perfect yet. I'm still convincing white men that there is much to gain from opening more seats at the table. But I am doing it from the table and that's progress. Or maybe it's a quota. But I'm finding peace in believing the former. Imposter syndrome has strangled my confidence at thirty events too many. I hope it's not something you ever have to learn the phrase for. I hope that the first time you hear 'imposter syndrome', it won't be a penny-drop moment explaining how you've been feeling. I might be wrong to wish it, but a small part of me also hopes that it will be the experience of a minority that you are no longer part of.

I doubt that I'll raise you in London, despite how diverse the adverts on TV are becoming. There's something changing. An attachment to the home we've known is splintering and my friends are slowly slipping back into the feelings of return that our parents were forced to suppress. We don't have to try to fit in anymore. At least, I don't want to want to, and I'm trying to lean into that. I'm welcoming the many ways my hair can show its versatility. I don't excuse the frizz anymore. I'm learning to speak Wollof. Broken English is kidnapping my jokes. I'm vacationing along the coast. Of Africa. We're having birthday dinners at Nigerian restaurants. We're spending too much money at Afro Nation. Again. I'm sending Burna Boy – Soke to corporate clients who have recognised how interesting everything about where I'm from is. Fela Kuti is being pulled into the same conversations as Bon Jovi. I can scroll down my Twitter timeline and laugh at African satire from the first generation diaspora in England. We are headlining shows and giving closing keynotes across the world. We are the new faces of multiple cultures and campaigns. We are owning things. We are creating movements and collecting funds. We are re-exploring and heading deeper into our roots. Pulling them to the surface and modernising them. And in doing so, I really like to think that we are welcoming our parents' youth back into their transitioned skin. My Mum still laughs at us sometimes when we ask her to make Pepper Soup when we're ill. She's still in the process of remembering that it coming before Sudafed or Calpol is reason to be proud. But the process is a beautiful one. There's a melancholic pace that allows much art to be created along the way. I've never been happier to be a writer, storyteller and commentator than today. It's a pleasure to track the transition.

The Japanese have this thing called *Kintsugi*. They believe that there is much value to be added in sewing broken pieces of pottery back together with gold. Perhaps if I had been raised to train my blackness's voice from a young age, the sheer elation that comes from screaming with my friends now wouldn't be the celebration that it always is today when we get together to chop or dance. Who knows. What I do know is that Mum's poem was one of hiding and finding a new version of herself to express, and then trying to teach that version to me. My poem was and continues to be a word on finding what my Mum had hidden, and then discovering how I can style that history today. My hope is that your poem will be one of wearing. I hope that your poem is a catwalk. I hope you will forever know little of your difference beyond how special your internal wiring is. I hope the world continues to become exactly as you imagine it to be as a little girl full of dreams. I hope you keep my Mother's eyes and Father's nose.

A Poem for Babygirl

And I hope that you learn to love them quicker than I did. I hope that what we are currently doing to each other on social media is undone before you take your first steps and I hope that you only see your temple for its glory and not its potential. I hope that you thank God for who he made you more than you question him about it. I'm sure that you will.

There is something in the air . . . actually, there is something in the black women around me that confirms that your poetry will be different to mine. Something in this year's Homecoming celebration in Ghana tells me that the rest of Africa is about to pull back the diaspora. Something tells me that the people you come to call neighbours will all look a bit more like you than my own neighbours did.

Initially I will sing you Nneka. And Burna.
And India Arie.
But then realise that you need less liberating.
Because baby girl
you will already be free.
You will write new poems,
And live new poetry.

TEMI MWALE

Yomi first came across Temi Mwale on one of the many TV screens in the Channel 4 newsroom, when she was working a late shift during her role as an online producer. She remembers being hugely moved and encouraged by her work. Following the murder of her childhood friend, Marvin Henry, Temi began campaigning for increased provisions to address youth violence. In 2012 she founded the youth-led organisation The 4Front Project. Her essay discusses how the failure to address the specific needs of young black people amounts to negligence and ultimately, to the violence we continue to see.

Building Peace:
The Case for Centring
Healing in our Approach to
Address Violence

For most of my childhood, I lived in Grahame Park Estate, North West London. Society's disdain for the 'council estate' is evident in the way it neglects and abandons these communities, and in its general disregard for those of us who live in them. When the connection to such an environment forms part of your identity, it is difficult not to *be* and *feel* marginalised from society. My childhood was shaped by the struggle that will be familiar to many others who began life in a similar community: poverty, violence and over-policing.

In 2012, aged 16, I set up The 4Front Project to provide young people who have lived experience of this reality with a platform to create change: change in our own lives, change in our communities and change in our wider society. Our mission is to empower young people and communities to fight for justice, peace and freedom. Over the last eight years we have been supporting those most impacted by serious violence and providing them with an opportunity to build peace at a national level. If we want to create a society that is not defined by young people killing other young people, we must address the root causes of this violence. Today, I write from my perspective as an experienced youth worker, racial justice campaigner and ultimately, a young woman affected by violence and injustice – determined to change the world.

As I reflect now, it is hard for me to fully articulate the impact that violence has had on my life. I experienced domestic violence in the home. I witnessed domestic violence in the homes of friends. I testified in court about the violence I had witnessed aged 11. I then started secondary school and walked through the very same school gates where 15-year-old Kiyan Prince had been stabbed to death only a year before. I spent the next few years collecting newspaper articles and reading everything I could about how serious youth violence was impacting the whole country.

Despite this research, during my teenage years I was incredibly detached from my own personal relationship to violence and the experiences that I continued to have whilst exploring the issue. I was assaulted by my first boyfriend, who dragged me down the stairs and pushed me to the ground when I was 15. Around this time, many of my friends became victims of sexual assault and rape. There was not a single day in our lives in which violence or the threat of violence did not feature.

There was a moment a few years ago when I sat down to think about all the violence I had ever seen or experienced growing up – it was overwhelming. I had never thought about all the incidents at the same time before. I did not appreciate the severity of my experience for a long time. This is a testament to the desensitisation that can occur when you are surrounded by violence. Often the gravity of your experience is not apparent to you. It is just normal. It becomes part of your life.

I can't remember too much about the evening of Tuesday, 26 October 2010. It was an unremarkable night. I had just celebrated my fifteenth birthday a few days before. How could I have known the relative innocence I possessed? That night I went to sleep completely unaware that my life was about to change forever. When I woke up the next morning, I found out that my childhood friend Marvin Henry had been shot. It was only a month before his eighteenth birthday. He lost his life.

Whilst I cannot summarise that morning in a way that would do it justice, I can say that I remember it vividly. Grief does that. I know for certain that many of us who have experienced loss will recall, in explicit detail, the moment our lives changed. I was hurled into shock, anger, and pain. Collecting all the newspaper articles in the world would not have made it easier to see Marvin's face on the cover of the *Evening Standard* that day. Nothing could have prepared me. Suddenly, it was real.

Prior to that moment, I had been emotionally impacted by the frequent killings of young, disproportionately Black boys. I had been moved to the point where I felt it was necessary to document their lives, collect evidence of their deaths and pursue my own search for solutions. I had been affected by a communal sense of loss and grief. But when Marvin was killed, it became personal. What I gained was an understanding of something that could not be translated through the research I had done: an understanding of the pain. It was visceral. Gut-wrenching. Heartbreaking.

Marvin joined a long list of teenagers who have been murdered by other teenagers in this country. I joined a long list of teenagers who have suffered bereavement. Hundreds of young people. Hundreds of families. Hundreds of communities. It is not possible to accurately measure the depth of impact that serious youth violence has on our society. Death is always a communal experience and when it is the result of natural causes, it is hard enough to deal with. A violent death creates an additional layer of pain – police involvement, media interest, court cases and more – all of which prolong the suffering.

If we are to gain a better understanding of the impact of violence on our communities, we must acknowledge that for many young people growing up in the UK today, the exposure to and threat of violence is woven into the very fabric of their lives. The murders are only the tip of the iceberg. Every day, young people become victims of violence and the majority of them survive. Being the victim of a serious attack in and of itself would be hard enough for most people. But what if you endure that experience but then continue to fear more violence every day? What if you're afraid, not only for yourself, but also for all of your closest friends? There are too many young people who fear that they might be killed every single time they leave their house. Unfortunately, this is not an unfounded fear. Violence is both irrational and unpredictable.

The level of stress and anxiety that many children carry with them, fearing for their personal safety and that of their friends, is simply unimaginable to most people. The tragedy is that young people who have been directly impacted by this kind of violence rarely receive specialist support to help them come to terms with their own victimisation. Despite the fact that they have had their sense of security and safety eroded, they receive very little assistance to deal with their pain.

If there is not adequate support in place for young people who have themselves been violently attacked, what hope is there that those of us who experience pain and trauma as a result of losing friends will be able to access support? This year, it will be a decade since Marvin was killed. In all that time, I do not recall anyone asking me how I feel, or how I am coping with his loss. I believe this to be true for most young people who have suffered bereavement in communities like mine.

The notion that many young people may be experiencing post-traumatic stress disorder is real. Yet even this doesn't adequately account for the fact that communities exposed to high and frequent levels of violence are not living *post* trauma. The opportunities for healing are few, because there is always another violent incident. Those of us who live in these environments endure extremely high levels of toxic stress. I can tell you firsthand that it is not only exhausting – it can be paralysing.

I believe that we live in a state of perpetual community trauma. This has contributed to a culture of desensitisation. Violence is perceived as normal, violence is expected and for the most part, violence is accepted. The notion that those of us who have been impacted by violence require specialist support should not be radical in this context. Aftercare is a form of prevention.

I can't help but conclude that the racialisation of this issue is partly why there is so little support available. Whilst it is true that violence affects young people across the UK, the fact that young Black men and boys are disproportionately the victims of this violence has been well documented. However, efforts to explain this disproportionality have failed to progress beyond the age-old racist narratives that seek to align violence, and crime more generally, inextricably with Blackness. As a result of this, young people who are not involved in crime at all, live with the very real threat and fear of criminalisation every day.

The policing I have witnessed in my community has allowed me to observe the additional harm created by an approach that relies solely on the criminal justice system to address social issues. This approach, which causes more harm than good, prioritises punishment and the notion of deterrence over tangible support. But we will not police our way out of this problem.

This approach does not seek to address the systemic issues which form the context for the disproportionate representation of young Black men as victims of serious violence. There is, of course, a wealth of evidence which highlights the multitude of complex factors that can contribute to violence. But a gap still remains for a nuanced account of the relationship between young Black people and serious youth violence.

It is crucial for us to understand the pervasive institutional racism that forms the very foundation of British society, and which is ever-present within the education and criminal justice systems. Black people are most likely to live in the most deprived neighbourhoods, Black children are disproportionately excluded from schools, the unemployment rate for young Black men is higher than for most other groups and Black people are disproportionately represented at every stage of the criminal justice system. This treatment is not new. This is an intergenerational problem. What has been done to address the institutional racism which was highlighted in the Macpherson report more than two decades ago? The lack of accountability for both historical and current failures has created a barrier which prevents young Black people from being able to rely on the very service that is supposed to protect them. Many feel unable to trust the police enough to call them, even when they feel scared and threatened, for fear of how they will be treated: not just by the police, but also by their own community.

How does the pathologisation of Black youth affect their ability to access care and support when they have been victimised? Who is entitled to victimhood? You may ask what purpose victimhood will serve. All too often in our communities the notions of strength and weakness may mean that most do not want to be perceived as victims. So, who are the victims? It is a fact that most young people who are 'perpetrators' of violence have themselves been victims of it. Rarely supported. Never healed. To understand this impact is not to condone violence, but to attempt to grasp why it happens. Young Black victims are routinely denied victimhood and are therefore denied the aftercare and support that victims are accorded.

'Crime' has become the predominant way in which British society views Black youth. Once criminalised, young Black people are only seen – and their experiences only understood – through this lens. This is not only distorted but also incredibly dangerous, as it prevents young Black people from accessing adequate support, offering them only punishment instead. Being victims of frequent state-inflicted violence as well as community violence can result in experiences of complex trauma. And this systemic oppression also plays a powerful role in the process of identity formation for marginalised populations. We need to better understand its impact on the self-awareness and perception of people in these communities.

In the UK, serious youth violence has become more prevalent over the last year, which has prompted renewed calls to increase the use of discriminatory policing tactics such as stop and search and gang databases. The 'gang' label has become a common tool used to deny victimhood. Living in a community like mine, you are suspected of criminality because of the way you look and dress. For some young people, becoming a victim of violence alone has been enough to earn them a place on a gang database. There is a lack of scrutiny and transparency over these databases – it is unclear how individuals end up on them and even more unclear how individuals can shed the label in the future. This has increased distrust between young people, the communities they come from and the police.

When my friend Marvin died and the media described his murder as the result of a 'gang feud', thus writing off his life, it added an extra layer of pain for those of us who mourned him. I was familiar with this binary reporting from all the articles I had previously read, written in the aftermath of many children's murders. They are either 'angels', and comments are solicited from their family, friends, teachers – anyone who can attest to the gravity of their loss; or they are 'gang members' and in these cases, when the loss means nothing more than statistics, it is the police and politicians who are invited to comment. Their lives become less meaningful, despite the fact that the descriptions of them are often unfounded.

British society has become obsessed with 'gangs' – arguably the 'folk devil' of our time – enabling what has been described as the 'gang industry' to develop and thrive. Tackling 'gang culture' has become a crucial way to access resources for policing and community funding and yet, it is also apparent that the 'gang' label has become synonymous with Blackness in Britain. As a result of this, young Black people who are affected by violence are dealt with through a criminal justice apparatus as opposed to an approach that seeks to meet their needs. Research has highlighted the questionable nature of gang policing, evidencing the erosion of human rights for those who are labelled.

With serious violence normalised not only by the everyday experiences of our children, but also by a society heavily invested in a violence industry, we cannot look to the 'gang' to explain violence. Furthermore, strategies that have sought to eradicate the 'gang' as a way of reducing youth violence have not worked. In 2011, David Cameron (then Prime Minister) announced in response to the riots in London and other parts of the country, that the state would wage an 'all out war on gangs and gang culture'. Nine years on, it is fair to say that the war has not been won, because we can't win wars against abstract terms. However, if we are to understand the 'war on gangs' as a war on Black youth, then the state is winning. The 'gang' label dehumanises young people, removing any right to victimhood they may have had and treating them simply as perpetrators.

Our criminal justice system is failing. I have spent hours in police stations, courtrooms and prisons, witnessing the misery inflicted on children who instead needed to be offered a sense of hope and the support to progress. Too often, they are not treated like children at all. Our prison system is in crisis. Prisons are not designed to rehabilitate: there is little support for the mental health epidemic, the drug trade is out of control, people are cut off from all support systems and can barely access educational opportunities. And violence is increasing. As Shauneen Lambe writes in the *Guardian*, 'a profit-based model of incarceration will measure success in profit. Only a therapeutic model will judge itself on therapeutic outcomes.' In 2017, the Chief Inspector of Prisons said that youth custody centres in England and Wales were so unsafe that a 'tragedy' was 'inevitable' and that 'not a single establishment inspected was safe to hold young people'. Locking up those who could be better helped by support in the community only exposes them to increased violence and reduces their opportunities when they leave. We do not need more punishment. We need more healing.

If we want to see a change, we have to do something radically different. Ultimately, the causes of serious youth violence are systemic. This conclusion frightens many, because it means that the vast majority of initiatives designed to address violence are inadequate. They fail to even attempt to change the infrastructure that generates violence in our communities. Unemployment and underemployment; homelessness and unstable living environments; unaddressed trauma; undiagnosed mental health issues; addiction; school exclusion; institutional racism and racial inequity are all issues which underpin the violence we see. And they are exacerbated by austerity policies that have made everyday life more difficult for those with the least. It is clear that our state is committed to marginalisation, poverty and inequality.

We need holistic, targeted support for those who have been most impacted by violence, including educational, mental health, legal and personal development support. We must invest in health and care, to ensure that young people access the support they need when they have become victims of violence and when they have been affected by it indirectly.

We must invest in youth and community workers. Many of us have dedicated our lives to this work because of our own personal experiences, but very few of us have space to deal with our own trauma and pain. We must provide both personal and professional support to support workers. We must train community members to be able to recognise mental health crises and learn tools and strategies to help people cope. This is not to replace therapists, but in recognition of the many barriers that exist to accessing this kind of formal support.

For young Black people, part of this holistic work is acknow-ledging the institutional and structural barriers they face, and the racial trauma they experience. Those engaging with them must be able to acknowledge the ways in which racism within society can accelerate the processes of criminalisation and limit the ability of some people to progress beyond criminalised identities. Further-more, there must be a thorough understanding of the impacts of pervasive criminalisation on members of communities experi-encing violence, whether they are directly involved in crime, or not. Young Black people urgently require services that can sup-port them to build their sense of identity in a society that is hostile towards them.

We must be braver. This is about way more than role models and youth clubs. Yes, the closure of youth facilities has been a direct attack on the safety of young people. Yes, young people rely on these safe places, where they can go and just be. But young people also need to be involved in challenging the systemic con-ditions that generate violence. Those who experience layered marginalisation are less likely to feel they have the power to create change. In order to support young people who are disenfran-chised, we must provide them with meaningful opportunities to learn how to stand up for their rights and create political change. The young people most entrenched in cycles of violence need a sense of purpose, not more punishment. They need more inclu-sion in society, not more exclusion and ostracism.

Instead of asking ourselves, 'How can we reduce violence?' per-haps we should ask, 'How can we build peace?' I believe that there is an important distinction between the two, not just in terms of focus, but approach. How often have we actually considered the concept of *peace*? This is about more than simply semantics. There has been no time in human history not marked by violence, and some might argue that the concept of peace is so far removed from reality it is never going to be attainable. But however aspirational it may be, if we are not bold enough to have this vision within our sight, then I argue that our attempts to reduce violence are relatively meaningless.

We should begin by asking ourselves: What would peace look like? What would peace feel like? What would make our young people feel safe? Only by answering these questions can we actually start the process of healing.

TONI-BLAZE IBEKWE

Toni is a force to be reckoned with in every sense. We have loved *Wonderland* magazine for years but our love for the fashion-forward publication only grew when we saw that a black British 90s baby, born to Nigerian immigrant parents, had been appointed editor. And she rose through the ranks from intern to Editor-in-Chief, no less. She is a talented stylist, working with the likes of Lupita Nyong'o, Jorja Smith, Nicki Minaj and Mary J. Blige, and also a talented writer, writing here about black women's continued deconstruction of stereotypes and the boxes society tries (and fails) to contain us in.

2020 and Beyond – The Black Woman V2.0

What's next? A question we ask ourselves at every level of existence, whether we are where we want to be or not. A question that, when applied to the position of the black woman in a post-Brexit, Donald Trump world, I am 100 per cent certain will elicit a different answer from every one of us.

At first, this question left me a little lost for words. Not in a negative way, but due to the uncontrollable levels of excitement I feel when thinking about how far we have come. What a decade it has been for black women! I hail from a generation in which (and this is sometimes still apparent) a dark-skinned woman can sometimes feel undervalued in the wide-ranging shade spectrum of black women. Ten years ago there was no #blackgirlmagic movement. I grew up as a young girl of Nigerian descent from South London, hair slicked to perfection, adorned with gems like the girls of HBO's *Euphoria* (we did it first!). I possessed the power to live and be proud of myself because of the values instilled in me by my mother and the women in my family.

Looking back, the attributes that were considered to make up 'blackness' for the black woman weren't always perceived in a positive light. For example, if I had been paid for every time I received an unwanted opinion from a bystander who interpreted my straight face as 'stooshe' and requested that I give them a smile, I would be a millionaire. At one point we were known for being 'rude' (but what that really meant was we were bold by nature) and 'ghetto' for our long nails, our ever-changing hair-styles and our slicked baby hairs. Fast forward a few years and these so-called 'ghetto' beauty trends are the ones we now see daily in the editorial pages of magazines and runway shows.

My point is, that at times the representation of the black woman in society has exasperated me, but while I am in no way saying we are now perfectly represented, I believe we have out-grown many of these negative stereotypes. We are multifaceted, and recognised as such, and this is thanks to the many women who have helped contribute to what I like to call 'Version 2.0 – The new black woman'. (It seems fitting to compare the new representation and face of the black woman to a software update, as we are constantly buffering and improving.) And so I want this essay to be a love letter to those who have been at the heart of the many triumphant moments in the last two decades that have brought us to this point.

Was the first of these moments when Beyoncé dropped 'Crazy in Love' back in 2003? When Jay-Z set fire to the car in her video, for me it felt symbolic of how unapologetically this powerful black woman was about to take the music industry by storm. Fast forward to Beyoncé's 2016 'Formation' video, in which – con-tinuing with her 'destroying cars' theme – we saw her laid out on a sinking police cruiser in the floodwaters of New Orleans: a visual denouncement of America's systematic racism. Or did our Version 2.0 begin with the emergence of fellow mogul and Bajan-born singer Rihanna, the feisty island girl from humble beginnings, who – as of 2019 – is the richest woman in music? A *black* woman.

2018 marked a pivotal moment in fashion, with Fendi's col-laboration with rapper Nicki Minaj – another boss, unapologetic in her approach, whom I admire. The collab was the first of its kind. Nicki, a strong, powerful black woman, taking up space in what has always been deemed the upper echelons of fashion, is further evidence of the changes in representation we've brought about as black women. And there are other iconic black women operating in the fashion space, such as stylists Missy Hylton and June Ambrose (who were stylists before it was deemed to be a legitimate career), without whom it wouldn't have been possible for those like myself to imagine ourselves there. Then there are women such as Lil' Kim, who redefined the use of sex appeal, taking ownership of it and using it to leverage her image – an image which still has a huge impact on pop culture styles today. The black girl magic continues, and, driven by the energy we as black women possess, like a trend, it is trickling down and spreading out across society. We are conquering each industry, one by one, like a game of dominos, forcing each of them to rethink their idea of the black woman.

I asked myself, 'What might the future hold?' when, in 2018, Anok Yai became the first black model in twenty years to open a Prada show (the only other model to do so was the icon that is Naomi Campbell). This moment further fuelled the conversation around tokenism in the fashion industry, with some focusing only on the fact it had taken twenty years for it to happen. But for me, Naomi's achievement was a vital part of the 'buffering' stage ahead of our V2.0, and Anok Yai's triumph was proof that we can't be held back anymore. Yai told vogue.com in 2018 'Me opening for one of the top fashion houses is a statement to the world – especially for black women – that their beauty is something that deserves to be celebrated.'

In 2015, Misty Copeland made history when she was promoted to 'Principal Ballerina' by the American Ballet Theatre: she is the first ever African-American woman to hold this title in the company's 75-year history. As a young girl growing up I could not have fathomed the idea of a black ballerina. She was not someone I had ever seen in the fairytale movies or represented on TV. I would have assumed that we were not 'soft' enough, or 'graceful' enough. Today, by contrast, little black girls all around the world have so many V2.0 role models visible to them, to aspire to and to emulate, as they go about creating who they want to be.

The greatest gymnast of all time is a 22-year-old young black woman, Simone Biles. She holds twenty-five world-title medals, more than any of her male or female counterparts. And her team-mate, Gabby Douglas is no stranger to accolades herself: she is the first American gymnast to win solo and team all-round gold medals at one Olympics and again, she's a black woman.

Representation across all industries is one of the most important building blocks there is, in aiding the growth and advancement of little black girls, and there have been so many recent highs in terms of representation of black women that, for me, they eclipse any negative commentary that might have trailed behind them. Take, for example, Halle Bailey of Chloe x Halle being cast as the little mermaid in the live-action movie of everyone's childhood favourite underwater rags-to-riches princess. Halle's casting as a character who is white in the animated movie caused a frenzy, with some critics demanding to know how a young black woman could portray a fictional character of a different skin colour. Funny isn't it? When you think that just recently *Harriet* screenwriter Gregory Allen Howard revealed that a studio head had once suggested Julia Roberts for the role of Harriet Tubman. 'Fortunately, there was a single black person in that studio meeting twenty-five years ago who told him that Harriet Tubman was a black woman,' Howard wrote in the *LA Times* in 2019. I like to think that in the 'call out' culture we live in now, a comment like this would not have been glossed over without consequences.

As I survey the landscape today I can see that there are so many 'firsts'. But I am excited that we are moving into a stage in which we will no longer be able to refer to a black woman's success as the first of its kind. Ultimately, *this* is what I believe is next for the black woman: our Version 2.0. As we excel in every industry possible, the phrase 'the first black woman to' will become redundant, and I cannot wait. In 1968, Saudra Williams became the first Miss Black America, the pageant was held as a response to the lack of racial inclusivity in the Miss America competition. As I write this, all four of the major beauty pageant top titles (Miss USA, Miss Teen USA, Miss America and Miss Universe) are, for the first time, being held by black women, with Zozibini Tunzi winning the Miss Universe title in 2019.

At this rate, the generation that comes next will look back and only see how high the bar has *always* been set for our achievements.

In 2019 in an article for ABC titled '"Why can't I be myself?":" Black women reject racism and embrace their natural hair' by Bakri Mahmoud, Dr Gatwiri, a lecturer in Social Science at South Cross University states, 'The last decade has been powerful in people rejecting the really insidious ways racism shows itself in being told the way your body must be.' I was struck by this quote because not only are we seeing a shift in black women's attitudes with regards to the policing of their appearance, but the same can also be said for the policing of our achievements and how we want to be represented and respected. Mahmoud writes, 'There are no strict rules or styles, but the idea is that, finally, black women are respected in their decision to represent themselves as they choose.' He is referring to hairstyles, but I think this also translates to how society deals with the black women (and how black women deal with society): there is a shift from acceptance to equality.

At the final of Miss Universe in 2019, Zozibini Tunzi in her closing address said, 'I grew up in a world where a woman who looks like me, with my kind of skin and my kind of hair, was never considered beautiful.' I can relate to this statement, even though I had so many beautiful positive black women in my family. As a young woman, sometimes society's pressures can feel stronger than the weight of our own instincts. But I know now that the generation that comes after me will not and should not bow to these pressures. With countless black women forcefully taking up space and cementing themselves in history positively, the possibilities for growth and self-belief are endless. I am so thankful for the many positive female figures who have come to the fore in the last decade or so. I am thankful for being chosen to take part in this anthology and to be able to share my view on where we are heading right now as black women.

We all want to keep pushing and breaking barriers together so we will no longer have to say that certain accolades are the first of their kind for us. When one black woman wins, it is a win for us all. Our journey now feels less like a competition in which we are pitted against one other. There is space for more than one token black girl in any field we occupy.

2020 and beyond for the black woman! We are in a relay race, passing the baton from woman to woman to advance.

YEMISI ADEGOKE

Yemisi is a former CNN Africa journalist, current BBC Africa reporter and Yomi's big sister. She describes Yemisi as her inadvertent writing inspiration (and also by becoming a journalist first, she dealt with all of the fallout from their Nigerian parents so Yomi didn't have to!). We have been fans of her work since we can remember (and Yomi is not just saying that because she loves her very much!). She's made several ground-breaking journalistic contributions, including participating in the Reading the Riots series in the *Guardian* in 2011 and unpacking the Fake News Crisis in Nigeria. We asked her to write this essay because we wanted to read something on the complicated relationship between the Diaspora and the motherland, and we knew she was the person to write it.

Homecoming

I was one of three black girls in my sixth form politics class and I was the 'loud one', a label I'd been christened with since primary school. I was comfortable with the identity I'd been given and back then I didn't think too much about the connotations of being a 'loud black girl', For me it was simple: I liked talking, I had opinions and I liked having them heard.

There was nothing more enjoyable to me than hijacking a boring lesson by turning it into a discussion about something, anything else. Intellectual back-and-forths, or as intellectual as you can be as a teenager, were fun for me. Not so much for my teachers, who made sure to note my propensity to talk and distract others in every class report.

Like most black teenagers born and raised in a country they're repeatedly told isn't really theirs, I was given several versions of the 'thrice as good' lecture by my parents, who always let me know my sex and race were strikes against me. Still, I was young, naive and optimistic enough to keep talking anyway, and my politics class was no different.

My class was exactly how you'd expect a sixth form politics class in the early 2000s to be: full of idealistic, curious teenagers, trying to make sense of the ever-changing world around them. It was my favourite class because, naturally, there were plenty of opportunities to have conversations and argue ideology. One day, we were discussing Africa, and one of the boys wondered why the continent was so poor. His tone was confident. He'd never set foot there, but he barely paused for breath as he reeled off his pick 'n' mix of the continent's stereotypes: mud houses, starvation, disease, war . . . I remember instantly feeling jarred. It wasn't just his smug confidence that irked me; it was the way he was talking about Africa.

As a Nigerian born and brought up in the UK, this type of negative stereotyping wasn't exactly new to me. I wasn't born when 'Live Aid' aired but grew up in its very long shadow. For my generation, Africa was the opposite of a cool. It was portrayed as a primitive, backward, war-torn monolith, where people spoke weird languages and had weirder names.

I've lost count of the number of times the African kids in my politics class would either band together to challenge what was being said, attempt to ignore or deflect it, and direct the heat onto something or someone else. But that day, as his stream of uninformed opinions continued uninterrupted, I could feel my temper rising. This was personal, and being the loud one, there was no way I could keep quiet. I looked over at the two other black girls in my class (who were also African), our eyes met in a sort of silent agreement and the three of us got 'in formation', taking down his points one by one. Our teacher, who was a good-humoured woman most of the time, let us argue for a little bit until we were pulled back into the lesson of the day. But the feeling that the 'dark and hopeless continent' trope had reared its ugly head didn't dissipate. I remember going home, still burning, as I relayed the whole exchange to my Mum.

In all honesty, the trope had never dipped its head to begin with. Centuries before 'Live Aid', the narrative of a primitive, war-torn, diseased and impoverished continent (or country as it's usually referred to) prevailed. If the Western media was to be believed, nothing good had ever come out of Africa, apart from maybe the animals, and even those were only good within the safe confines of a safari park or as a trophy on a wall.

The late Kenyan writer Binyavanga Wainaina challenged this myopic characterisation in his 2005 satirical essay 'How To Write About Africa' which touched on the many ways Western reporters and writers continuously get the continent wrong. He advised would-be authors to 'treat Africa as if it were one country', and not to 'get bogged down with precise description. Africa is big: fifty-four countries, 900 million people who are too busy starving and dying and warring and emigrating to read your book.'

Little under a decade later, Amy Harth's paper, 'Representations of Africa in the Western Media: Reinforcing Myths and Stereotypes', shows little has changed. Harth lists a series of myths and stereotypes that shape media coverage, including myths of lack of progress, lack of history, poverty, population, hopelessness and so on. Harth goes on to state that these myths and stereotypes are largely accepted because 'when the media presents a story, it is not merely a story, but *the* story. The media's role in representing Africa is definitive. It's because of this role that they have the power to reinforce myths and stereotypes, which might otherwise be difficult to sustain. Their misrepresentation becomes the primary or only representation of the continent.'[1]

That afternoon, in class, my teenage self had been confronted by these lazy tropes yet again, and again I wanted to challenge them. Since my words hadn't worked, I thought that pictures might. My Dad was doing some work in Angola at the time and we had some brochures around the house showcasing beautiful homes and skylines in Luanda. I spent all of that evening compiling a collection of these brochures, eagerly looking forward to the next day's confrontation. I was determined to show my classmate the 'positive side' of the continent; it wasn't all sadness, wasn't all disease, wasn't all war. But in the end, he only shrugged as he looked through the brochures: it wasn't that serious to him. But it had always been serious to me and it continued to be; whenever I heard negative reports about the continent, I'd try and counter it with stories about something positive.

By the time I finished my post-grad degree, eight years later, it looked like certain sectors in the Western world were beginning to look at Africa differently. Some African countries were experiencing strong economic growth, which led to a stream of stories highlighting the continent's emerging middle class, the spread of the Internet, mobile phones and later, social media. People seemed excited, hopeful even. In 2000, *The Economist* ran a cover story proclaiming Africa as 'the hopeless continent', using every trope available. Eleven years later, the magazine changed its tune: 'Since *The Economist* regrettably labelled Africa "the hopeless continent" a decade ago, a profound change has taken hold.'

Now, the magazine declared, Africa was rising.

For Africans in the diaspora, like me, this shift in perception simply proved what we'd been saying all along; there's a lot more to the continent than you think. The speedy adoption of social media 'back home' helped push the 'Africa rising' narrative even further. More people that looked like us, were sharing their own realities of the continent with the world, without having to go through the gatekeepers of the Western press or the gaze of eager voluntourists.

For me, this opened up a new dimension to my relationship with my country of origin. I'd been to Nigeria a handful of times, but it was always for some kind of family event. I had little to no concept of the country outside these heavily sheltered and short trips, but now, for the first time, through social media I was able to see what fun without the family looked like. And honestly, it looked amazing. Instagram Nigeria was the epitome of the 'Africa they don't show on TV': beautiful beaches, beautiful people, beautiful smiles. Why wasn't anyone showing this side of the country?

There was also an interesting trend: young people were choosing to leave the diaspora to move to Nigeria. For some, moving back to Nigeria had always been part of the plan, the diaspora was simply a place to get an education or some work experience, but Nigeria was home. But for others, like me, it wasn't. We'd never lived in Nigeria before, but suddenly found ourselves diving headfirst into moving there.

I'd never considered it before until my Dad, who had moved there a few years earlier, suggested it after my first solo trip to Lagos. A friend and I had visited the city, and it was the first time I'd seen it on my own terms. It felt brand new, so exhilarating and so different from home. I couldn't stop talking about it when I got back. But the idea of actually moving there seemed outlandish, at least at first. It wasn't exactly practical: I didn't know anyone in Lagos apart from my Dad and a handful of family members, I didn't have a job, I didn't know the system, I had no friends there. I'd essentially have to start from scratch.

But the opportunity to do something different was so tempting. I was a journalist, trying to change the world through telling stories. The one-dimensional scope of reporting on Africa hadn't changed enough for my taste and by going back I could contribute to the narrative shift: showing more of the good and not the bad, echoing Harth's idea that 'African news must also challenge the stereotypes and myths which cause current coverage to misrepresent Africa.'

According to my Dad, lots of young people in the diaspora were moving back and doing well for themselves, why couldn't I? So I did. It was exhilarating, but at the same time extremely overwhelming. I quickly learned that being a Nigerian in Croydon, South London, is not the same as being a Nigerian from Croydon in Lagos, Nigeria. It took me slightly longer to dig deep into my place in Nigeria's social hierarchy. In the early days it felt so nice not to have to constantly navigate daily microaggressions that I didn't think much about it. When I first arrived, a tight-knit community of 'returnees' – one of many names given to people who relocate – helped me settle in. They showed me what Lagos life was like beyond Instagram.

They were people who had moved back from the US, from Canada and Europe, and of course their motivations varied. Some came back by choice, others by force, some had never lived in Nigeria before, others had left to get educated and had always planned to return. Some came back to explore the country, others to expand their horizons, but most came to tap into the vast opportunities we'd all been told about: economic, social, or simply being able to take advantage of the weaknesses of a corrupt system and thrive. There were also some returnees who wanted to 'save' Nigeria. Armed with big ideas, naiveté and boundless enthusiasm they moved back because they were compelled to change things, to make a difference.

I fell into this category and wanted to do my bit through my storytelling, but I soon learned Nigeria didn't need positive stories, what it needed was balanced and nuanced ones. Storytelling that acknowledged the flaws, faults and challenges (ignoring them simply diminishes the majority for whom these things are a reality), but that also shows the hundreds of other things that make up the tapestry of the country. Just as the US and UK are not defined by just one thing, Nigeria, and other African countries shouldn't be either, they should be afforded the same benefit as other countries and have their whole story told.

The naiveté and optimism of many returnees isn't necessarily a bad thing. There's no harm in trying to change any environment for the better but I'm worried about an uncomfortable dynamic emerging. Returnees are forming a sort of new elite. There is an important caveat here, not all returnees are created equal – there is of course the ruling class of Nigerian elite. The son of a billionaire businessman who went abroad to do a Masters, and a girl who grew up in a working-class home in South London, do not necessarily move back to the same version of Nigeria. The latter may not have the immediate connections, knowledge of the country or the capital to hit the ground running, but the two are bound by the perception that they're at a level above almost everyone else. And this perception is problematic.

It reminds me of the Biblical parable, 'The Prodigal Son'. We, the returnees had gone abroad and 'enjoyed' all the spoils of the diaspora. Meanwhile, our father, Nigeria, had been waiting patiently, full of hope for us to return home, and now we had. In those first few years, each time I met an older person (especially one affiliated with the establishment) and they found out I'd relocated, they reacted joyously. 'It's people like you we need in this country,' they'd say, even when they knew very little about me. Their joy had nothing to do with me, but more to do with what they thought I represented.

In the Biblical story, the father tells his servants to give his returning son his 'best robe, a ring for his finger and sandals for his feet'. Then he instructs them to kill a calf and throw a feast. There aren't robes and calves for us, but we are rewarded. Even for returnees who start from scratch, like I did, there's scratch and there's *scratch*. Foreign accents alone make it easier for people like me to gain access, which is valuable currency in Nigeria. Irrespective of whether you're actually qualified or not, it helps get a foot somewhere in a door that is otherwise firmly shut; if you happen to be qualified, a degree from a foreign institution, it means more respect, better jobs, better wages and a speedier climb up the ladder.

Returnees are positioned as the hope the country needs, free of the corruption that has infiltrated everyone else. Having experienced the world beyond Nigeria, it is understood that we know how things are supposed to be, and we can make them so. To make matters worse some returnees not only buy into this idea but actively strive to replicate and enforce the classist and oppressive structures that exist on the ground. Rather than push for change, as the returnee mantra goes, they are quite happy to be absorbed into the status quo and to ascend to the top of the food chain.

This is not to say there aren't people who have moved back who are exceptionally qualified, with many things to offer, who have done and continue to do excellent things; there are many. It's not to say either that there isn't a role for returnees to play in the development and progress of Nigeria; there is. What that role is, I don't quite know, but I do know Nigeria doesn't need 'returnee saviours'.

The idea reinforces the dangerous myths identified by Harth. One that immediately springs to mind is the myth of a lack of progress: the idea that Nigerians living in Nigeria have done nothing to try to improve the current state of affairs and they therefore need returnees to swoop in and save the day. This kind of erasure totally dismisses the ongoing work and efforts of people for whom moving to other countries is not an option. For them, Nigeria is the only reality that exists.

I remember a would-be returnee talking passionately about how much she wanted to kickstart a 'real' feminist movement in Nigeria, because the country seemed to be making such little headway in the fight for women's rights. While the latter part of that sentence is true, nothing she was suggesting was different to what hundreds of thousands of women in Nigeria had been diligently doing for decades. Why did she not want to join and support them? People who were already knowledgeable, familiar with the terrain and all the ins and outs of the country?

This behaviour carries echoes of the white saviour 'gap year' trope that we have criticised for years. Someone with little knowledge of a country decides they want to go there and start an initiative: perhaps it's teaching young people how to read, or some kind of health drive or another noble cause. There's nothing intrinsically wrong with this, but at times it comes with the assumption that 'these kinds of things don't exist, and only I can do them'. In most cases this simply isn't true. There are lots of people doing or trying to do these things, they have the experience, they have the knowledge, they may not be perfect but that's where partnership and collaboration comes in, working with these people instead of erasing them.

In the Biblical parable, while the prodigal son was off living life, the father's other son remained with him. He worked hard in the fields, doing what was expected of him. When he sees how his father treats his brother upon his return, he grows angry and confronts him. His father tries to explain, but in the Bible it's not clear whether either the two sons or the son and his father ever reconcile. Similarly, some Nigerians are, understandably, not thrilled with the presence of a burgeoning new elite. Life is already difficult enough: they are facing a struggling economy, mass unemployment, little opportunity and now a new set of people appear and make their life harder, even if it is inadvertently.

The rising resentment is palpable: snide comments about people with accents or foreign degrees, the questions about whether or not returnees are running from something, the law or failure. If you're a returnee and you're yet to feel any of this then you haven't been paying attention – and you should. So then what's the solution?

I guess it's a cop-out to say I don't know, but I don't. As minorities in our home countries, we are constantly asking people to check their privilege, as we should and as they should. As a black woman existing in the world, I never thought I'd be in a position where I have to check mine, but as a returnee living in Nigeria, I realise I do.

References

1 Amy E. Harth, 'Representations of Africa in the Western Media: Reinforcing Myths and Stereotypes' (Master's Thesis, Tiffin, OH: Tiffin University).

Contributors' biographies

Abiola Oni

Abiola Oni is a Nigerian-British writer based in London. In 2016, her short story *75* won the *Guardian* and 4th Estate short story prize for black and minority ethnic (BAME) writers in the UK. Her other short stories have been published internationally. She is currently working on her first novel.

Candice Brathwaite

Candice Brathwaite is a 'mummy blogger', influencer and founder of 'Make Motherhood Diverse' – an online initiative that aims to encourage a more accurately representative and diverse depiction of motherhood in the media.

With a background in marketing Candice quickly grasped the power and potential that Instagram had to offer and began to share her family life on the platform – her partner Bodé (Papa B), daughter Esmé-Olivia and baby son RJ – keen to show that young black families weren't just surviving but thriving.

Candice is the creator of *Teatime!*, a five-minute, daily Instagram story 'show', talking about her own life and tackling the bigger issues too. *Teatime!* has since become a sell-out live event series.

Candice has worked on multiple campaigns and has several ongoing partnerships (Pampers, Dove, Specsavers and Weight

Watchers to name just a few) and appeared on countless panels, including Stylist Live and a debate at the Hay-on-Wye Literary Festival about modern motherhood.

Candice has also been featured in or contributed to the *Metro*, *Huffington Post*, *Red Magazine* and *Stylist Magazine* and has appeared on BBC News, Channel 5 News and Radio 4.

Her first book, *I Am Not Your Baby Mother* is published by Quercus.

Charlie Brinkhurst-Cuff

Charlie Brinkhurst-Cuff is a journalist, editor, features writer, columnist and creative with focuses on race, lifestyle, travel, media, youth culture and social politics.

She is the Head of Editorial at *gal-dem*, a writer and former editor at *Dazed* and a *Guardian* freelancer. Charlie has written columns for the *Observer, ipaper* and *Metro* and writes freelance for a variety of publications, including *easyJet Magazine* and the *Financial Times*. She is an experienced panelist and speaker on radio and TV and her commercial clients include Exposure, Nike and Channel 4.

Winner of the 2017 Georgina Henry Award for Innovation in Journalism, Charlie is also a Scott Trust Bursary alumna.

She is the editor of *Mother Country: Real Stories of the Windrush Children*, a leading new exploration of the Windrush generation featuring David Lammy, Lenny Henry, Corinne Bailey Rae, Sharmaine Lovegrove, Hannah Lowe, Jamz Supernova, Natasha Gordon and Rikki Beadle-Blair.

Elisabeth Fapuro

Having graduated with an arts degree in literature, Elisabeth converted to law in 2015 working within financial services and is a Future Trainee Solicitor at an international US law firm. As a black woman from an underrepresented background in law, Elisabeth has worked closely with a number of the UK's largest diversity organisations in order to help widen access for other junior professionals of African and Caribbean descent entering the legal profession. @elisafaps for both Instagram and Twitter.

Eunice Olumide

Born in Edinburgh, Scottish supermodel Eunice Olumide has worked across the world, walking the catwalk for legendary designers including Mulberry, Alexander McQueen, Christopher Kane and Harris Tweed and appearing in editorials via *New York Magazine*, *Vogue* and *Harpers Bazaar*, among many others.

Olumide is the host and producer of the *Sista Collective*, the UK's first ever podcast dedicated to women of colour, on which she interviews world heavyweights in film, fashion and television. An active philanthropist, she has spent much of her career fundraising for charities and working with big brands to support their own charitable endeavours.

In 2018 she released her best-selling book, *How To Get Into Fashion*, which highlights her work in sustainability, diversity and preventing exploitation in the fashion industry and in August 2019, she was invited to speak at the Edinburgh International Book Festival. Olumide is also an actress, and has sold out shows at both the Edinburgh Fringe and the Apollo Theater in New York.

A passionate activist and campaigner, she has also worked with the Centre for Social Justice and spoken at the Houses of Parliament influencing the first ever inquiry into the impact of fast fashion on the environment. In 2019 she created 'Next Generation Regeneration' curating exhibitions, talks and events at Tate Modern and the V&A.

Fiona Rutherford

Fiona Rutherford is a British journalist, news editor and social producer, born to first-generation immigrants from the Caribbean.

In 2018 Fiona joined Bloomberg News to help launch its new 24-hour streaming product Quicktake. Her work on the product, as well as her input around shaping Bloomberg's global diversity and inclusion strategy, led her to be a finalist in the Black British Business awards rising star category for media. In 2019, she was relocated to New York City to continue her work at the company's headquarters in Manhattan.

Fiona, who holds a BSc in Psychology and Neuroscience and an MSc in Psychology, launched her career in journalism through winning a science-writing scholarship with the *New Statesman* magazine.

She has written stories and edited for several publications including *BuzzFeed News*, *GQ* magazine and the *Financial Times*. Fiona is best known for her reporting on UK inequality and social justice issues. She was one of the first journalists at the scene of the Grenfell Tower fire and her on-the-ground reporting helped set the news agenda around the tragedy. She has also written investigative pieces around disability rights, discriminatory nightclubs and a controversial medical condition blamed for deaths in police custody.

Jendella Benson

Jendella is a British Nigerian writer, head of editorial at *Black Ballad* and the author of 'Young Motherhood'. Her photography has featured in the *Guardian*, the *Metro* and the *Voice* newspaper, and has been exhibited across the UK and internationally.

Kuba Shand-Baptiste

Kuba Shand-Baptiste is a commissioning editor and columnist on the *Independent*'s Voices desk. She typically covers news, politics, pop culture and social justice, and has written for the website since 2016. She has also written feature, news and opinion articles for the *Guardian*, *Black Ballad*, *Metro*, *VICE*, Self.com, *gal-dem*, *Stylist*, *Ladybeard*, *Dazed*, the *FT Adviser* and more.

Kuchenga

Kuchenga is a writer, a journalist and an avid reader of black women's literature as a matter of survival.

She is a black transsexual feminist whose work seeks to cleave souls open with truth and sincerity.

She has been published in many online magazines including *Vogue* and *Harpers Bazaar*.

She chooses to live wherever her heart leads her. She is proud to be called a 'lady of letters' and a 'woman of wanderlust'. In the years to come she hopes to follow in the footsteps of Marie Daulne and Johny Pitts to see if she can become a true 'Afropean'.

Twitter: @kuchengcheng and Instagram: @kuchenga

Nao

Neo Jessica Joshua, better known as Nao, is an English singer-songwriter and record producer from East London. Her sound has been described as soul combined with electronic music, funk and R&B. Nao coined the term 'wonky funk' to describe her style. She released her debut album, *For All We Know*, in 2016, and her second album, *Saturn*, in 2018.

Paula Akpan

Paula Akpan is a journalist, speaker and co-founding director of Black Girl Festival, an arts and culture festival celebrating Black women, girls and non-binary people through a large-scale annual event and year-long initiatives.

A sociology graduate from the University of Nottingham, Paula's work – journalism and through her festival – mainly focuses on race, queerness and social politics and she regularly writes for a variety of publications including *Teen Vogue*, the *Independent*, *Stylist*, *Bustle*, *i-D*, *Al Jazeera* and more.

Phoebe Parke

Phoebe Parke is a social media editor and digital journalist specialising in culture and lifestyle. Born in London to a Jamaican mother and English father, she holds an undergraduate degree in English and German Literature from the University of Warwick, and a Master's degree in journalism from Brunel University. Parke has written extensively about race, celebrity and viral trends for publications including CNN and *Grazia*.

Falling in love with the Internet back when you could throw a sheep on Facebook, she has been using her storytelling skills to manage and grow social media accounts since the age of 19. Now, she shares her commentary on social issues and uses her platform to dispel common misconceptions around online communication.

Princess Peace

Princess Ashilokun (aka Princess Peace) is a 21-year-old black-British Nigerian poet who has been highly praised for her poignant wordplay, skilled delivery and ability to place societal issues under a new light. Often writing on themes advocating for social justice, she aims to spread her belief that in order to change the world, we must first become the change we wish to see in it. Her aim for her poetry is for it to be 'The sound of a revolution not yet born'. She studied English Literature and Language at Oxford University.

In 2017, Princess Peace was recognised as part of the top forty emerging poets around the UK by the Roundhouse, and was commissioned by Powerful Media to perform at the 2017 UK Top 100 African-Caribbean Influencers dinner, as well as the 2018 Aleto Foundation Charity Ball. Princess Peace has also performed for The Huntley Archives and the BCA, as well as touring up and down the country as a guest performer at a number of universities.

Selina Thompson

Selina is an artist and writer whose work has been shown and praised internationally. Her practice is intimate, political and participatory with a strong emphasis on public engagement, which leads to provocative and highly visual work that seeks to connect with those historically excluded by the arts.

Selina's work is currently focused on the politics of marginalisation, and how this comes to define our bodies, relationships and environments. She has made work for pubs, hairdressers, toilets and sometimes even galleries and theatres, including BBC Radio, the National Theatre Studio and The National Theatre of Scotland as well as theatres across the UK, Europe, Brazil, North America and Australia.

Selina has been described as 'a force of nature' (*The Stage*), and 'an inspiration' (*Independent*). She was featured in *The Stage* 100 Most Influential Leaders 2018, and awarded the Forced Entertainment Award in 2019.

Siana Bangura

Siana Bangura is a writer, producer, performer and community organiser hailing from South East London, now living, working, and creating between London and the West Midlands.

Siana is the founder and former editor of Black British Feminist platform, No Fly on the WALL; she is the author of poetry collection, *Elephant*; writer of the play, *Layila!*; and the producer of *1500 & Counting*, a documentary film investigating deaths in custody and police brutality in the UK. Siana works and campaigns on issues of race, class and gender and their intersections and is currently working on projects focusing on climate change, the arms trade and state violence.

She is also a workshop facilitator, public speaking trainer and social commentator. Her work has been featured in mainstream and alternative publications such as the *Guardian*, *Metro*, *Evening Standard*, *Black Ballad*, *Consented*, *Green European Journal*, *The Fader*, and *Dazed*. Her past television appearances include the BBC, Channel 4, Sky TV, ITV. And most recently *Jamelia Presents . . . The Table*.

Across her vast portfolio of work, Siana's mission is to help move marginalised voices from the margins, to the centre.

Sheila Atim

Sheila Atim is a London based actor–musician. She has appeared in *Othello* (Shakespeare's Globe), *Girl From The North Country* (Old Vic and Noël Coward Theatres) for which she won Best Supporting Actress in a Musical at the 2018 Oliviers and The Critics' Circle Award for Most Promising Newcomer.

She was also nominated for the Emerging Talent Category at the 2017 *Evening Standard* Awards. Other theatre includes *Les Blancs* (National Theatre) and the *Shakespeare Trilogy* (Donmar Theatre), for which she received Equity's Clarence Derwent

Award. Other theatres include the RSC, The Coronet Theatre and the Finborough Theatre.

Her screen work includes *The Pale Horse* (BBC1), *The Feed*, *The Underground Railroad* (Amazon), *The Irregulars* (Netflix), *Harlots* (Hulu) and *Bounty Hunters* (Sky). Her film roles include *Bruised*, *Sulphur and White*, *Twelfth Night* and *The Show*. Her radio work includes *The Anansi Boys* (BBC Radio 4).

Sheila wrote the stage play *Anguis*, which debuted at the 2019 Edinburgh Fringe festival. She has also written music for *The Etienne Sisters* (Theatre Royal Stratford East), *Doubt: A Parable* (Southwark Playhouse) and *Time Is Love* (Finborough Theatre).

Sheila was made an MBE for services to drama in 2019.

Sophia Thakur

Combining honest and provocative lyrics, Sophia is known to many as 'our generation's first poetry influencer'. With over 14,000 YouTube followers, performing at universities, Glastonbury and TEDx, Sophia Thakur is one of the most recognisable figures in UK performance poetry today. Her charming and gentle wisdom married to her thought-provoking storytelling ability has led her to touch millions of lives both on and offline.

Sophia's first published poetry collection *Somebody Give This Heart a Pen* (Walker Books) takes readers on an intimate journey through love, loss, faith and self-discovery, Sophia gives voice to the experiences that connect people and encourages readers to look into themselves and explore the tendencies of the heart.

Temi Mwale

Temi Mwale is a racial justice campaigner and the Founding Director of The 4Front Project, a member-led youth organisation empowering young people and communities to fight for justice, peace and freedom. She focuses on fighting against institutional racism and is passionate about working towards a world where we use a radically different approach to resolving conflict within society. Her work at The 4Front Project has changed the way that people understand how to support young people who have been affected by violence. The organisation has also shaped the agenda around how to tackle the systemic causes of violence. Temi pioneered an approach that empowers the young people most directly harmed by violence and the criminal justice system to be at the forefront of a grassroots movement for change. She has used her legal background to design and deliver a series of legal education programmes to support marginalised young people to drive change. Temi grew up on Grahame Park Estate in North West London. It was her early experiences of injustice that formed her primary motivation to create change. She studied Law at the London School of Economics and Political Science where she was a High Spen Scholar.

Toni-Blaze Ibekwe

A 90s baby born in London to Nigerian parents, fashion has always been in Toni-Blaze Ibekwe's blood. With her grandmother owning her own tailoring business, her flair for fashion started at a young age, accompanying and assisting her mum and grand-mother in tailoring and designing.

Her first experience began with creating her own collections at a young age, drawing strong influences from McQueen, with his grandeur and his ability to always stand out. This is reflected in her work, creating timeless imagery with photographers and directors both on an international and national basis.

Graduating from Central St Martins with a 2.1 in fashion communication, Toni Baze joined *Wonderland* magazine as an intern and quickly proceeded up the ranks, now holding the position of Editor-in-Chief.

Toni-Blaze has developed a fan base for her unique style and her ability to bring out the wow factor in her a-list clients, who include Lupita Nyong'o, Jorja Smith, Mary J. Blige and Camila Cabello.

Yemisi Adegoke

British born and bred, but Nigerian by heritage, Yemisi Adegoke is a multimedia journalist for the BBC, currently based in Lagos, Nigeria. A graduate of the Arthur L Carter Institute of Journalism at New York University, Yemisi moved to Nigeria with a strong desire to be a part of a narrative shift in the way stories about Nigeria and Africa in general were told. She has written and produced for a number of media organisations including CNN, *Quartz Africa*, the *Guardian* (Nigeria), the *Guardian* (UK) and *TRUE Africa*.